THE INTIMATE GARDEN

THE PHOTOGRAPHY OF

TREVOR CRONE

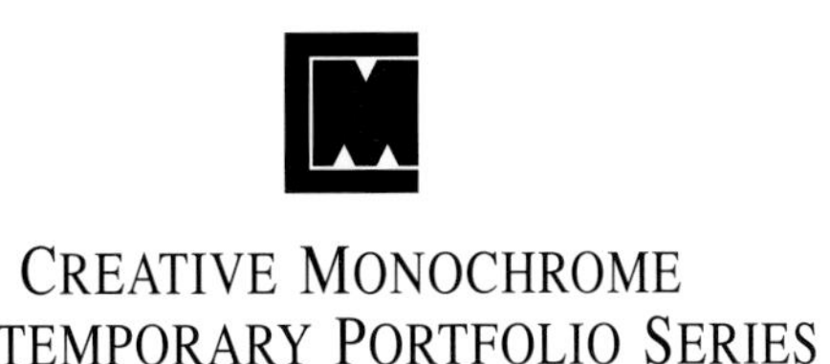

CREATIVE MONOCHROME
CONTEMPORARY PORTFOLIO SERIES

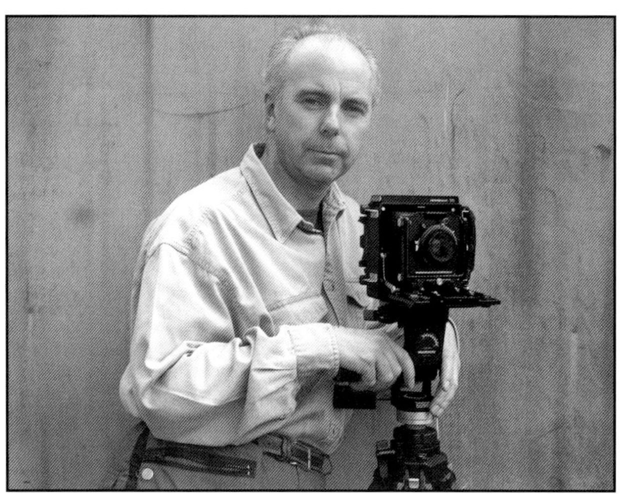

Photograph: Angela Crone

TREVOR CRONE first bought a camera in 1973, mainly with the intention of recording his daughters growing up. As a school laboratory technician, he was quick to learn about darkroom work and this fed his enthusiasm, which was reinforced by joining Greenwich photographic club in 1977. He has read widely on the subject and has particularly enjoyed the works of Ansel Adams, Edward and Brett Weston, and Wynn Bullock. By the mid-1980s photography had become a passion, and he rapidly acquired recognition as a highly creative worker of great technical skill, reflected in his growing interest in medium and large format work. His work has been published in several magazines, books and calendars and as greetings cards and postcards. Working primarily in monochrome, Trevor has acquired considerable expertise in the use of infra-red film and has prepared a technical booklet on this subject for Creative Monochrome.

DEDICATION

In memory of Frank and Peggy

THE INTIMATE GARDEN

The photography of
TREVOR CRONE

Published in the UK by Creative Monochrome Ltd,
20 St Peters Road, Croydon, Surrey, CR0 1HD.

British Library Cataloguing-in-Publication Data:
A catalogue record for this book is available from the British Library.

ISBN 1 873319 28 2
First edition, 1996

Printed in England by Penshurst Press, Buckingham House,
Longfield Road, Tunbridge Wells, Kent, TN2 3EY

ACKNOWLEDGEMENTS

Thanks to my photographic companions on many trips to Kent, Dave Mason and Keith Cox, and to my wife Angela, who has become a 'photographic widow' and has shown infinite patience while waiting with me for the light to change.

Introduction

Trevor Crone

Being a Londoner born and bred, the fields and coast of Kent have always been accessible to me, both as a child and now as an adult with my own family. Revisiting old haunts has rekindled childhood memories: intimate images of windblown reeds, quiet woodland glades, the fun and discovery of rock pools.

I can remember as a child going hop picking with my parents and grandparents along with hordes of other pickers from London's suburbs. And there are fond memories of Sunday and bank holiday day trips spent playing family ball games on the beaches and greens of Kent's coastal resorts – picnics by the sea eating delightful tomato and sand sandwiches (so that's why they call them sandwiches); still, dad always bought me an ice cream to stop me crying.

Kent's resorts were then the Riviera for London's holiday-makers, although as the years roll by people seem wealthier and more and more travel abroad, mainly using the Kent resorts for weekends and trips. However, many Londoners seem to like to retire to Kent's accessible coastal towns.

Whilst I love Kent, I'm equally frustrated by it. For so much of Kent's fine fields and woodlands are strictly private and access is denied. Although I don't condone trespass, I do believe in the freedom to roam providing one takes care not to cause any damage. As the environmental maxim goes, 'take only photographs, leave only footprints'.

Kent may not have the grand, extrovert landscape of Wales or Scotland, but it does have an introvert, intimate landscape. For me, the beauty and appeal of Kent is in moving closer with my camera to study and enjoy the details which represent the essence of the county, rather than standing back to take in the sweeping view.

I just have to photograph. It has become a way of life for me. Even if I don't do anything with the negatives, I just love to go somewhere to take pictures. I'll photograph anything that appeals and communicates with me at the time. Sometimes the subject matter is obvious, immediately significant; at other times the photography is more intuitive and the image will communicate more fully at a later date. It is these images that are often the more rewarding: they tend to be more subtle and hold deeper significance.

I feel that to be successful in photography you must become one with your subject. Then the photography becomes intuitive, a form of meditation. You relate to the subject's form, texture, and the light it reflects: you feel it as well as see it. It's during such moments and intense quietness that a completeness is felt – one is reluctant to leave the subject. You feel you have witnessed something special, something magical. I hope the images in this portfolio will convey to the reader this same special feeling.

PORTFOLIO

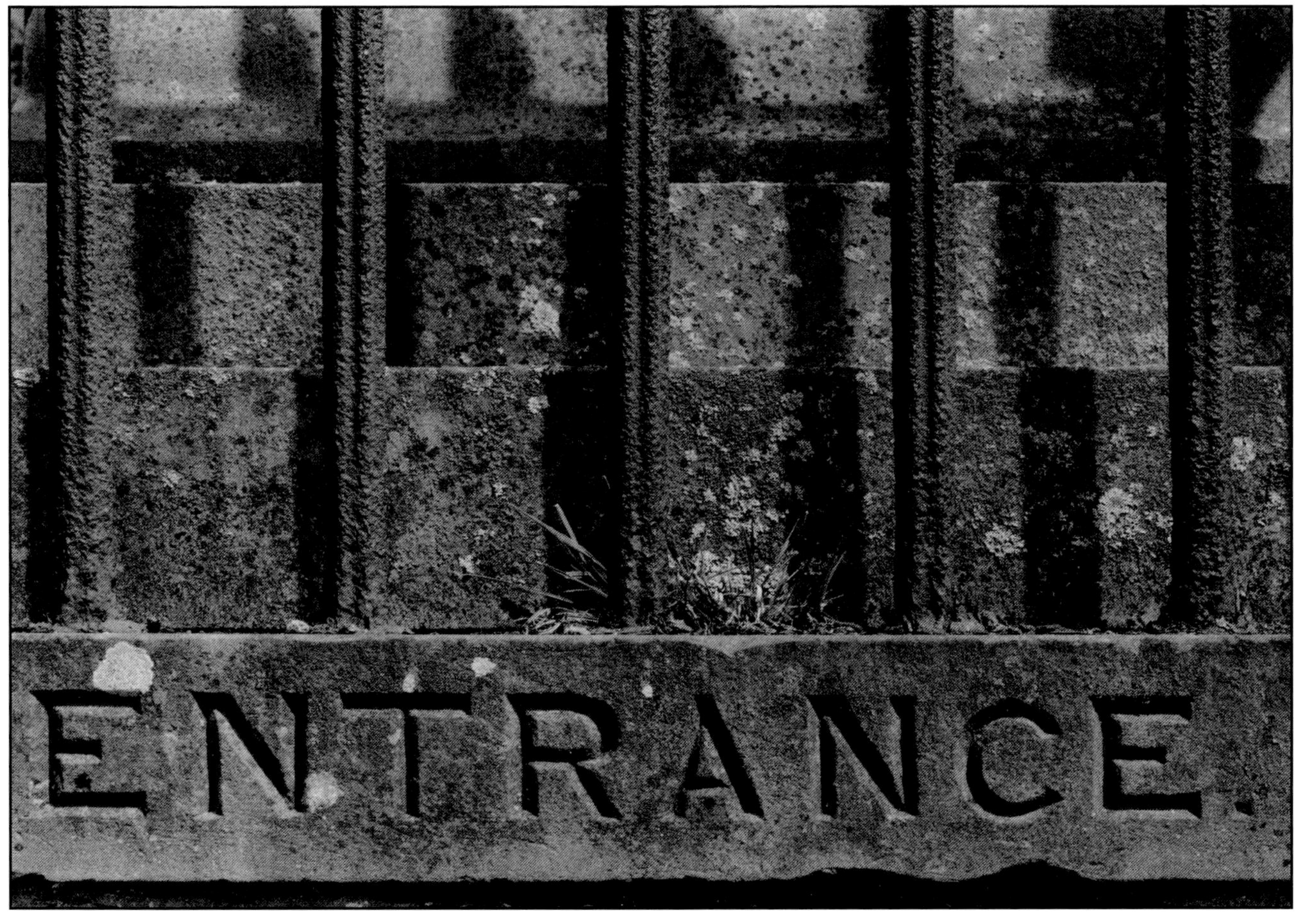

1

Entrance

Tomb detail, St Michael on the Hill, East Peckham, 1995

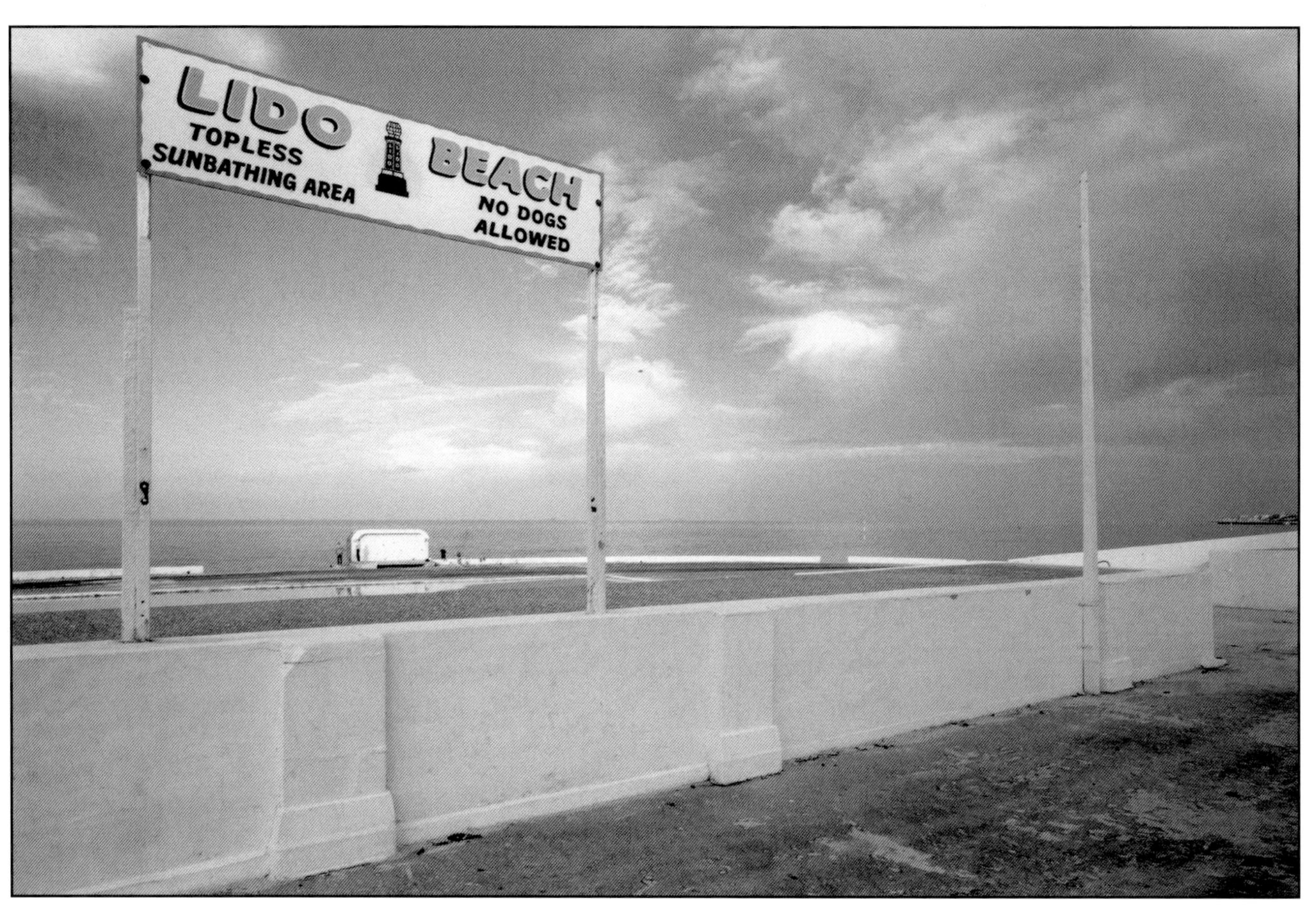

2

Lido beach

Cliftonville, Margate, 1994

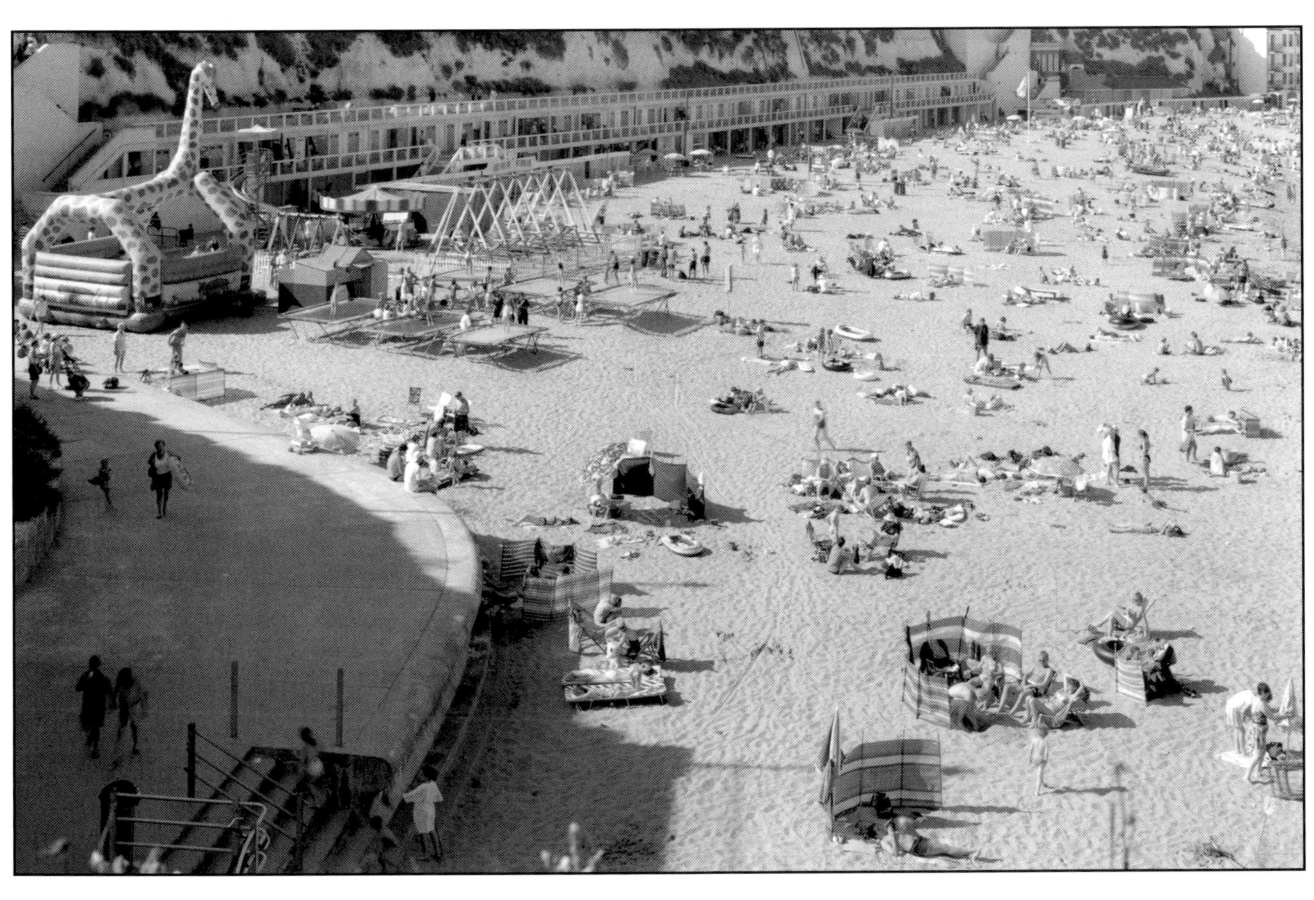

3
Height of summer
Viking Bay, Broadstairs, 1995

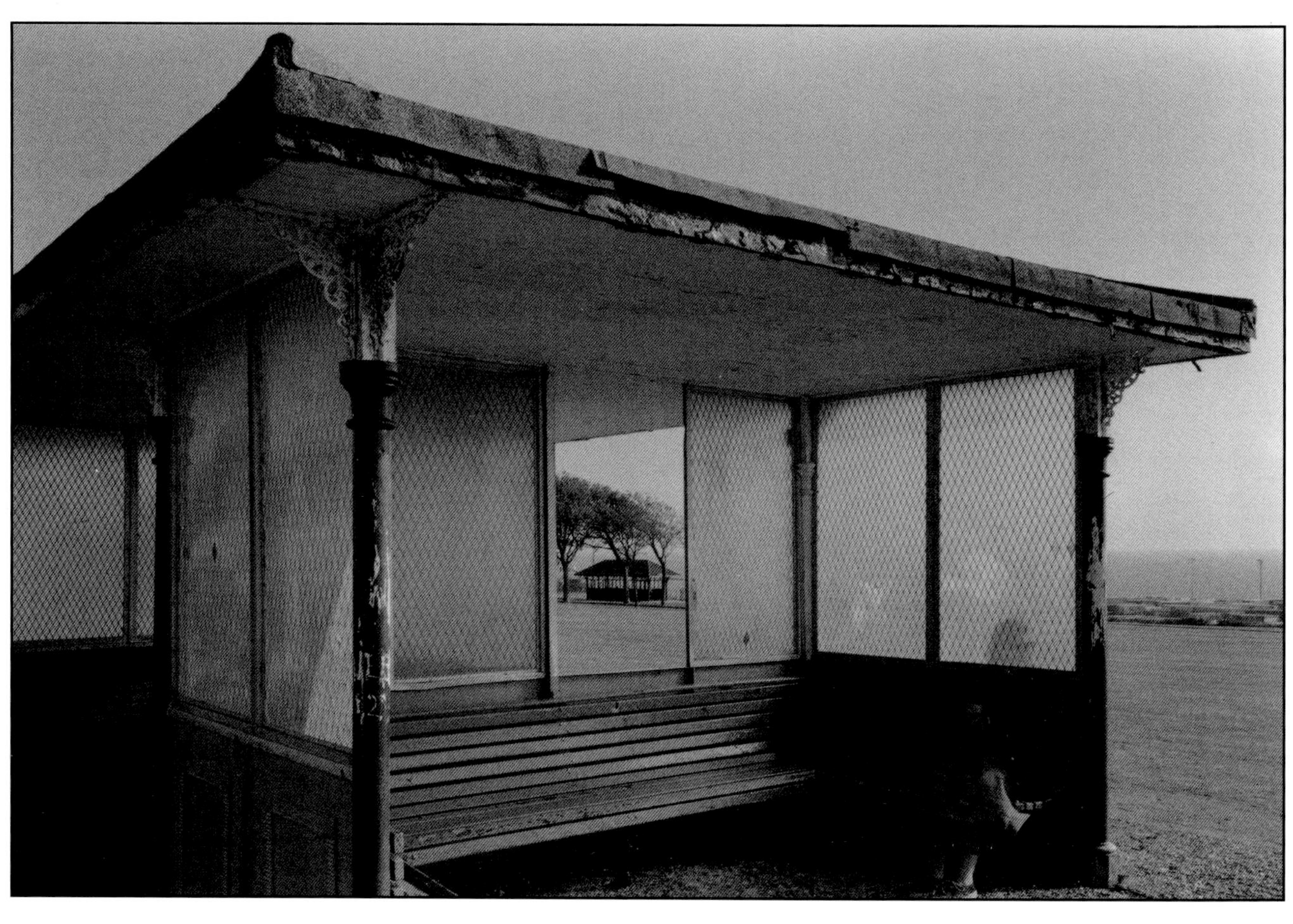

4
Shelter
West Cliffe, Ramsgate, 1995

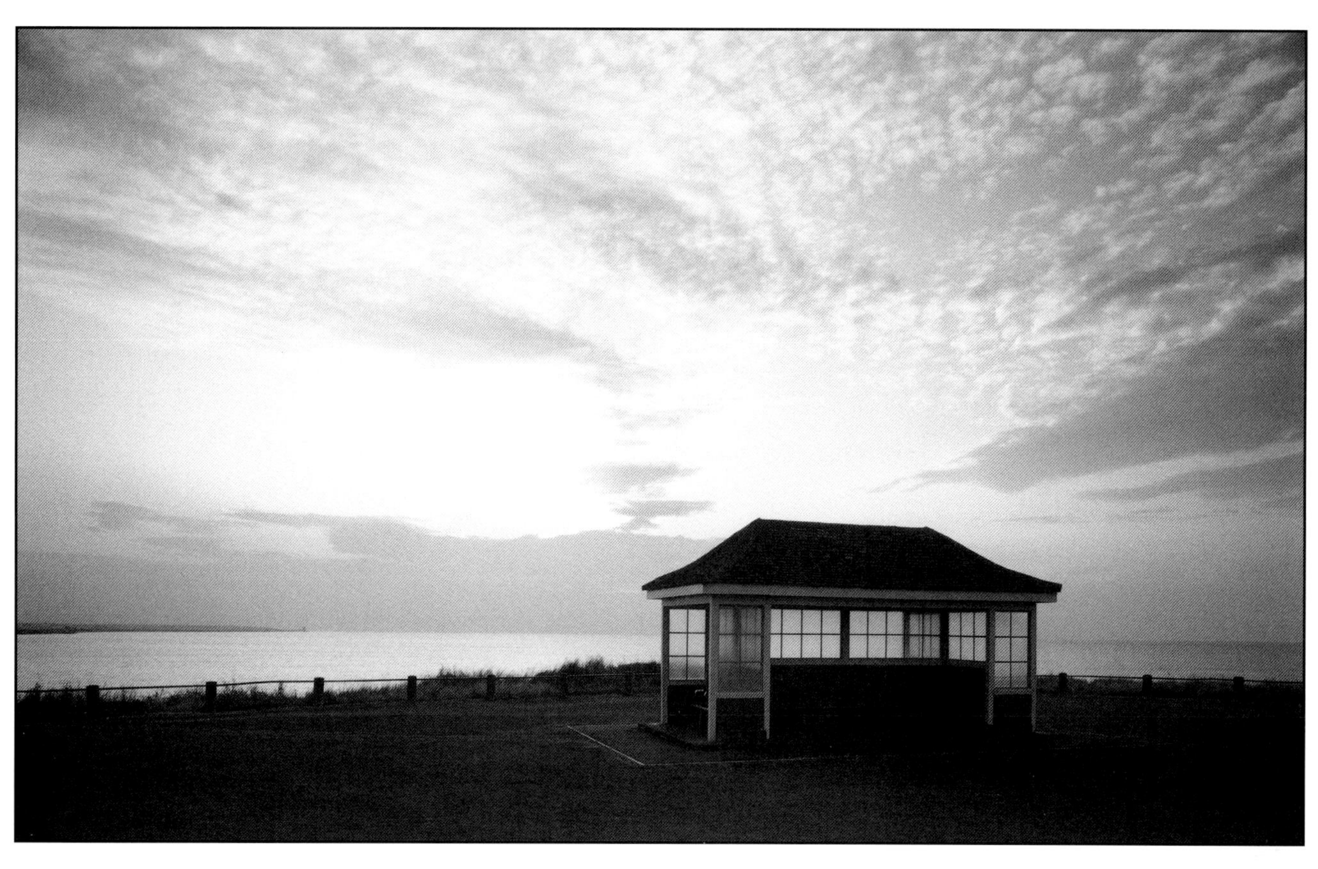

5
Shelter
Minnis Bay, 1994

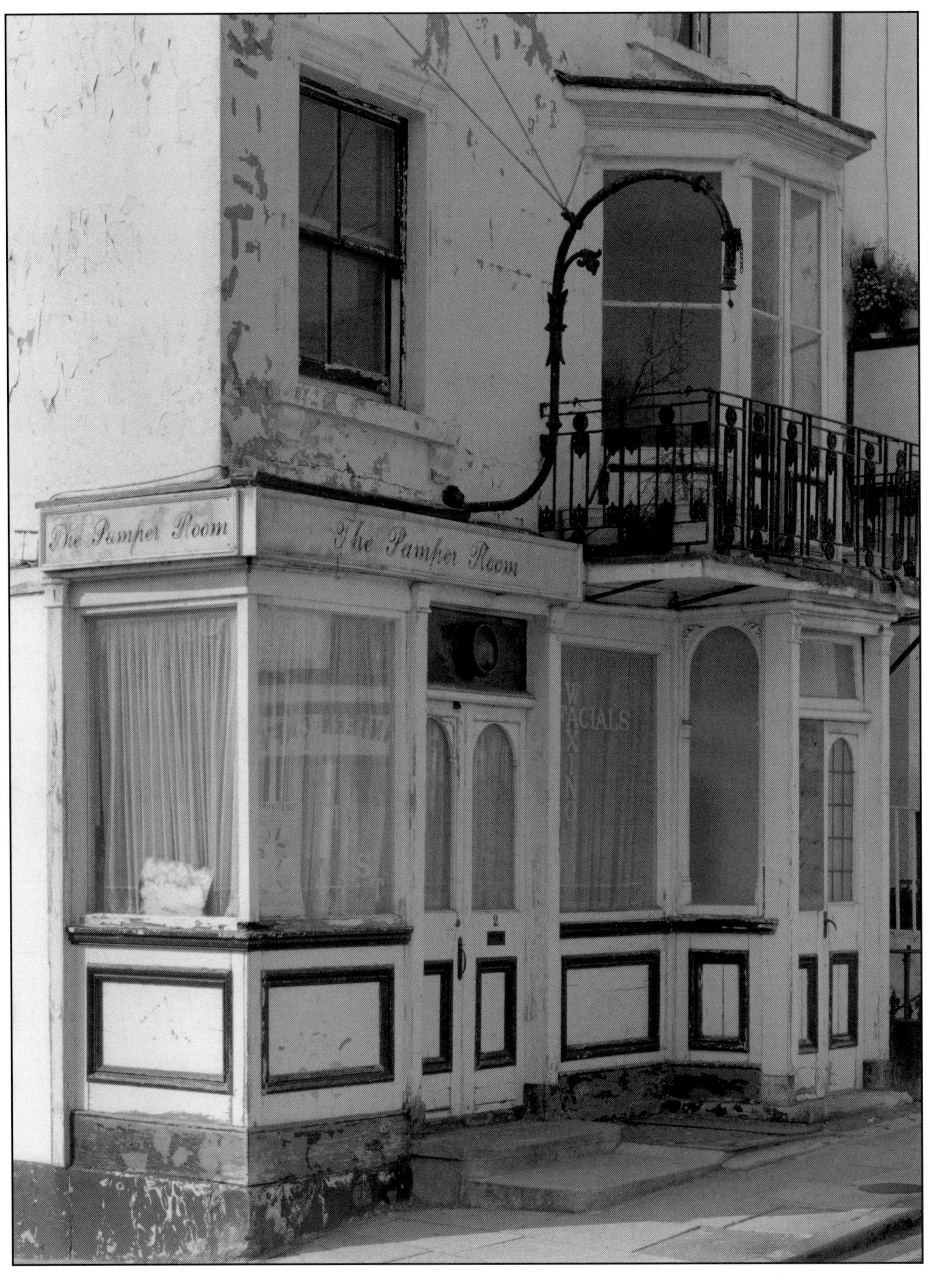

6
The Pamper Room
Ramsgate, 1995

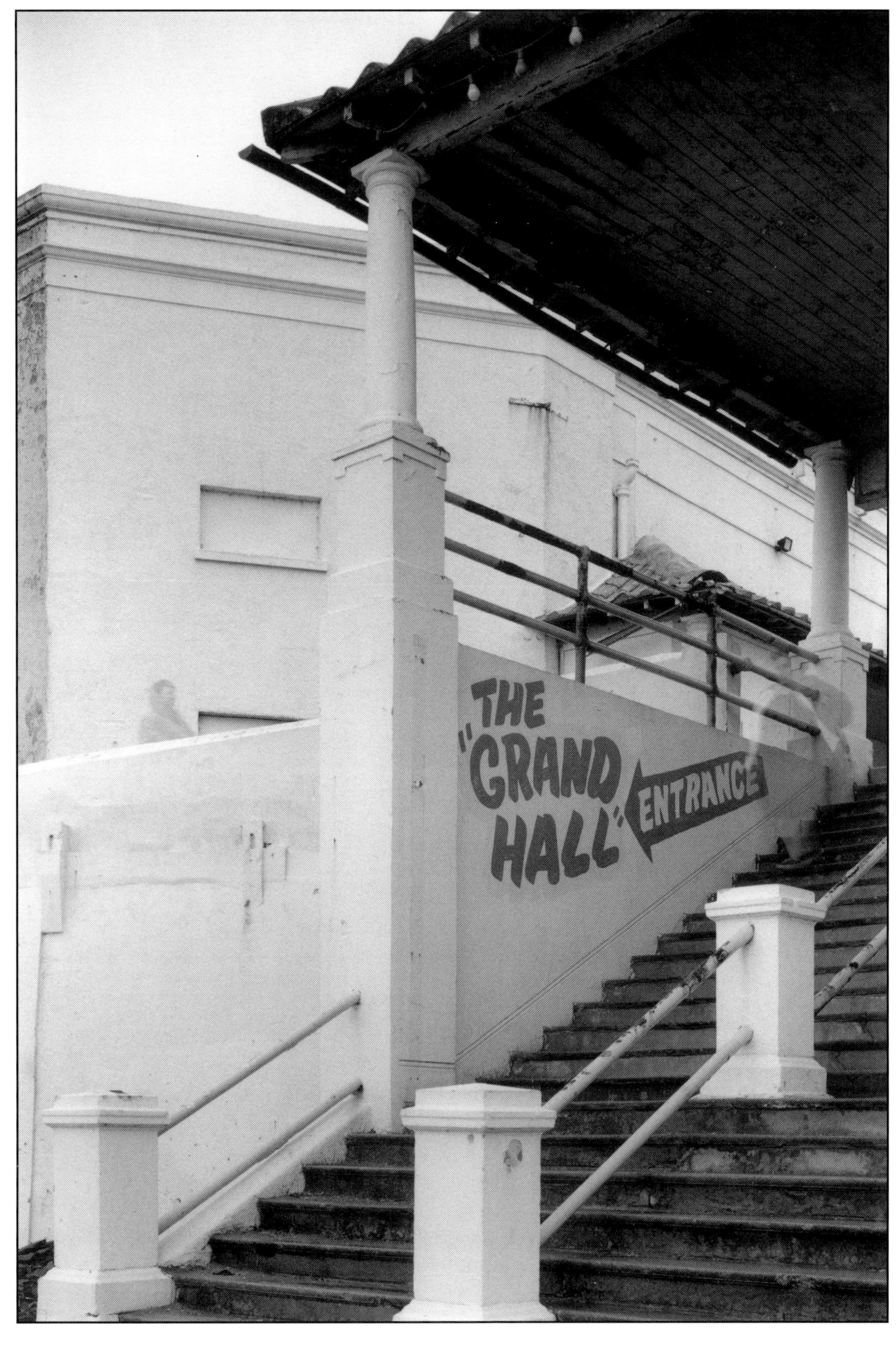

7
Lido leisure centre
Cliftonville, Margate, 1995

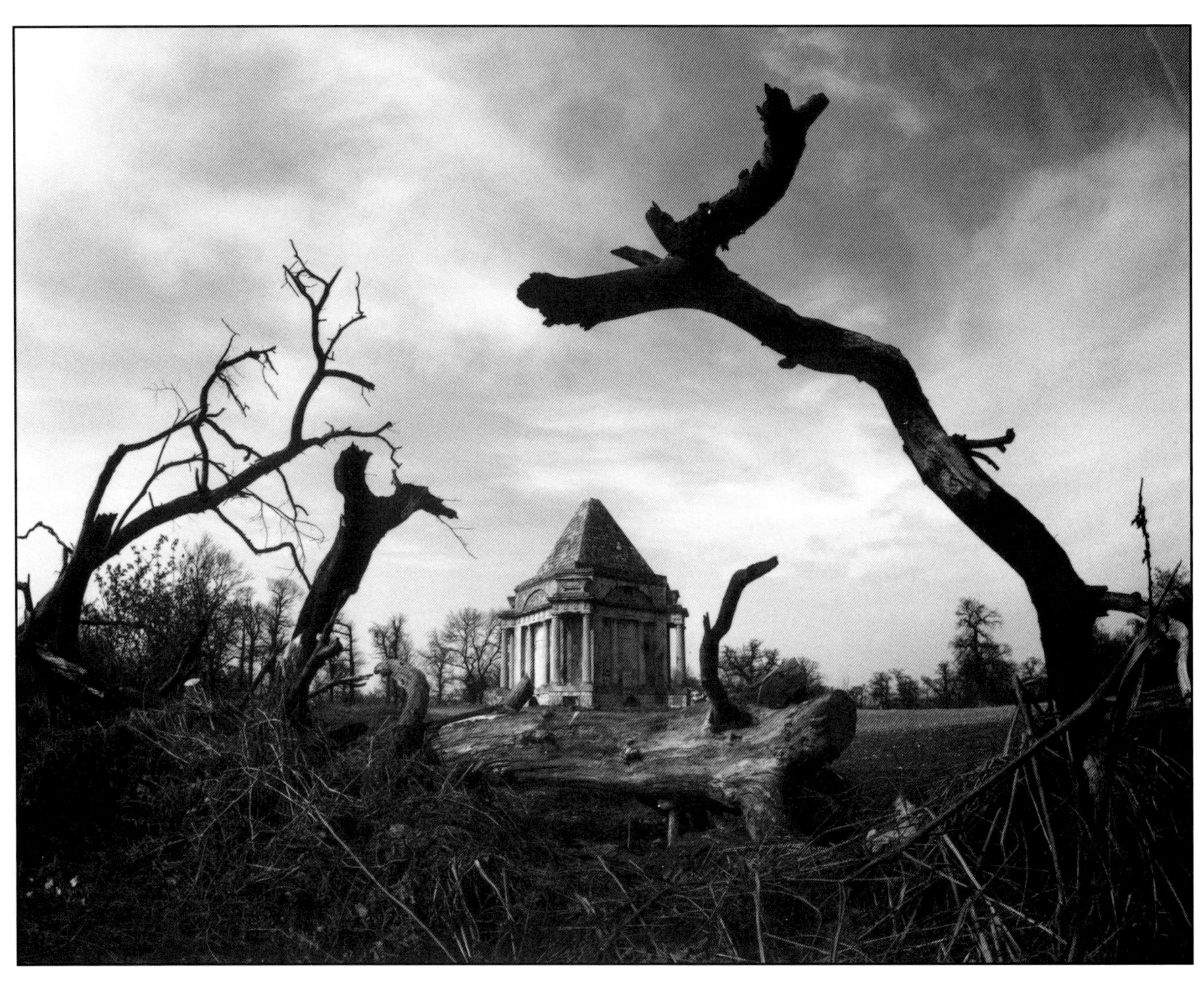

8
The Mausoleum
Old Deer Park, Near Cuxton, 1993

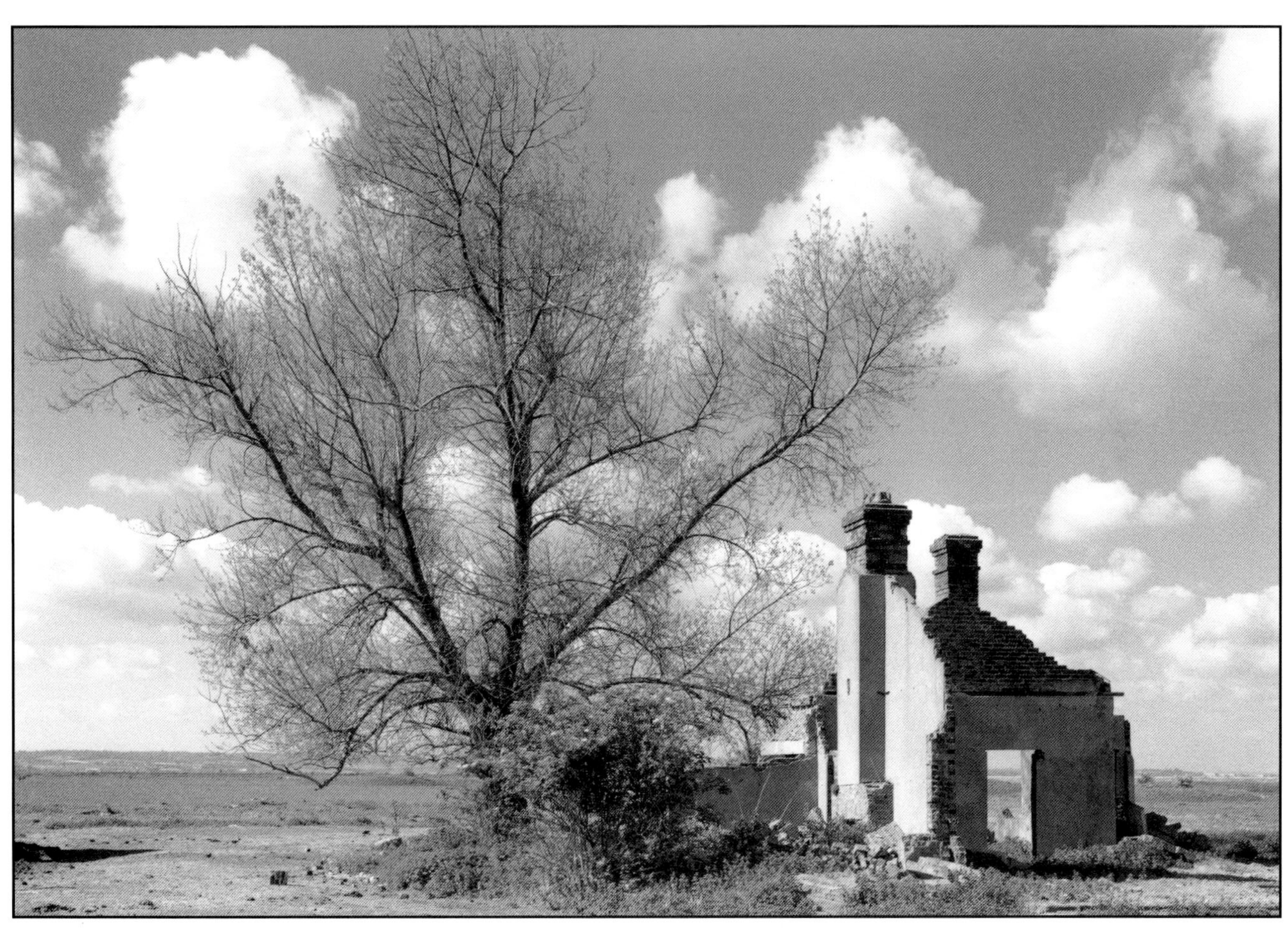

9
Broken homestead
Cliffe Marshes, 1995

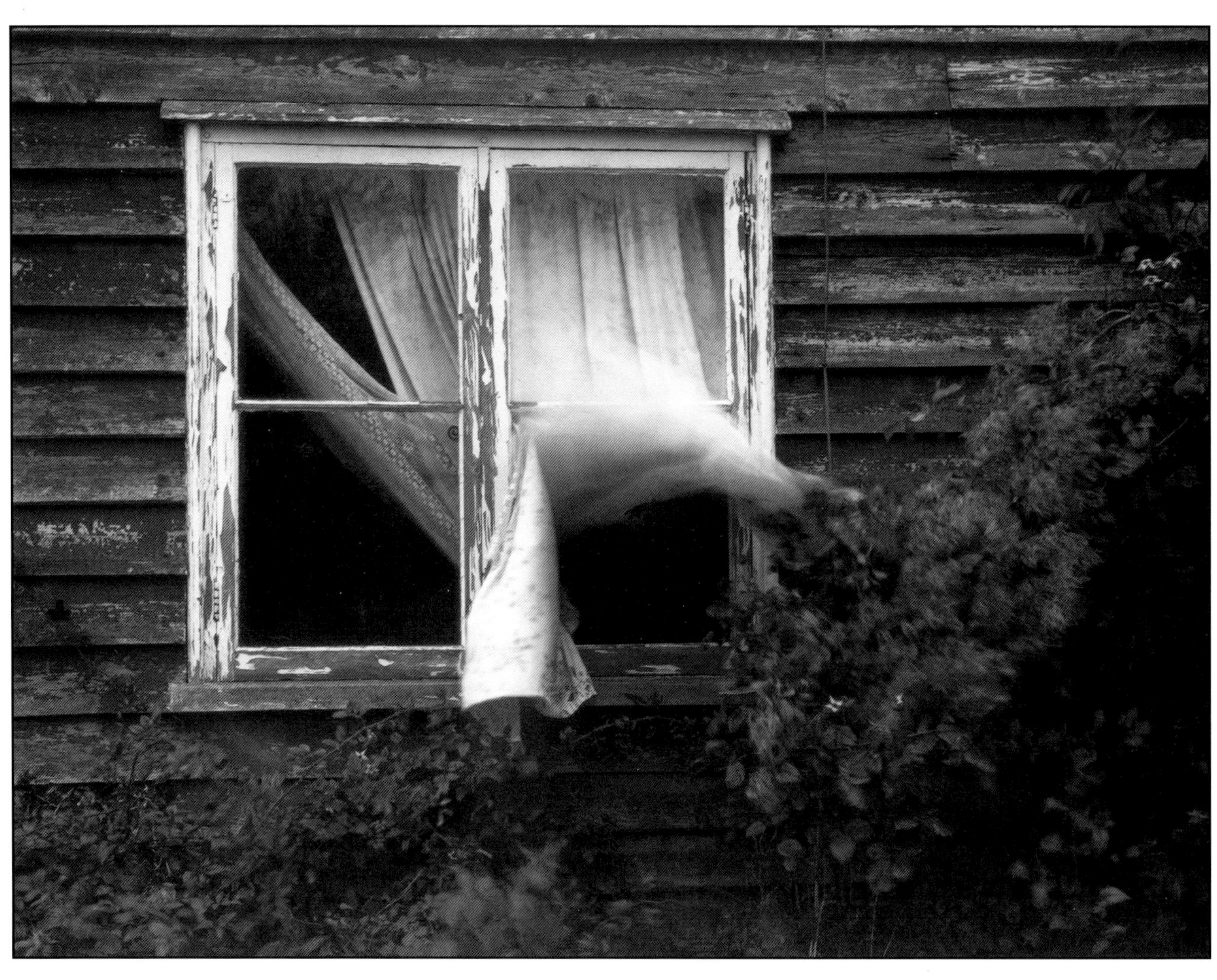

10

Sinister window 1

Derelict house, Near Burham, 1990

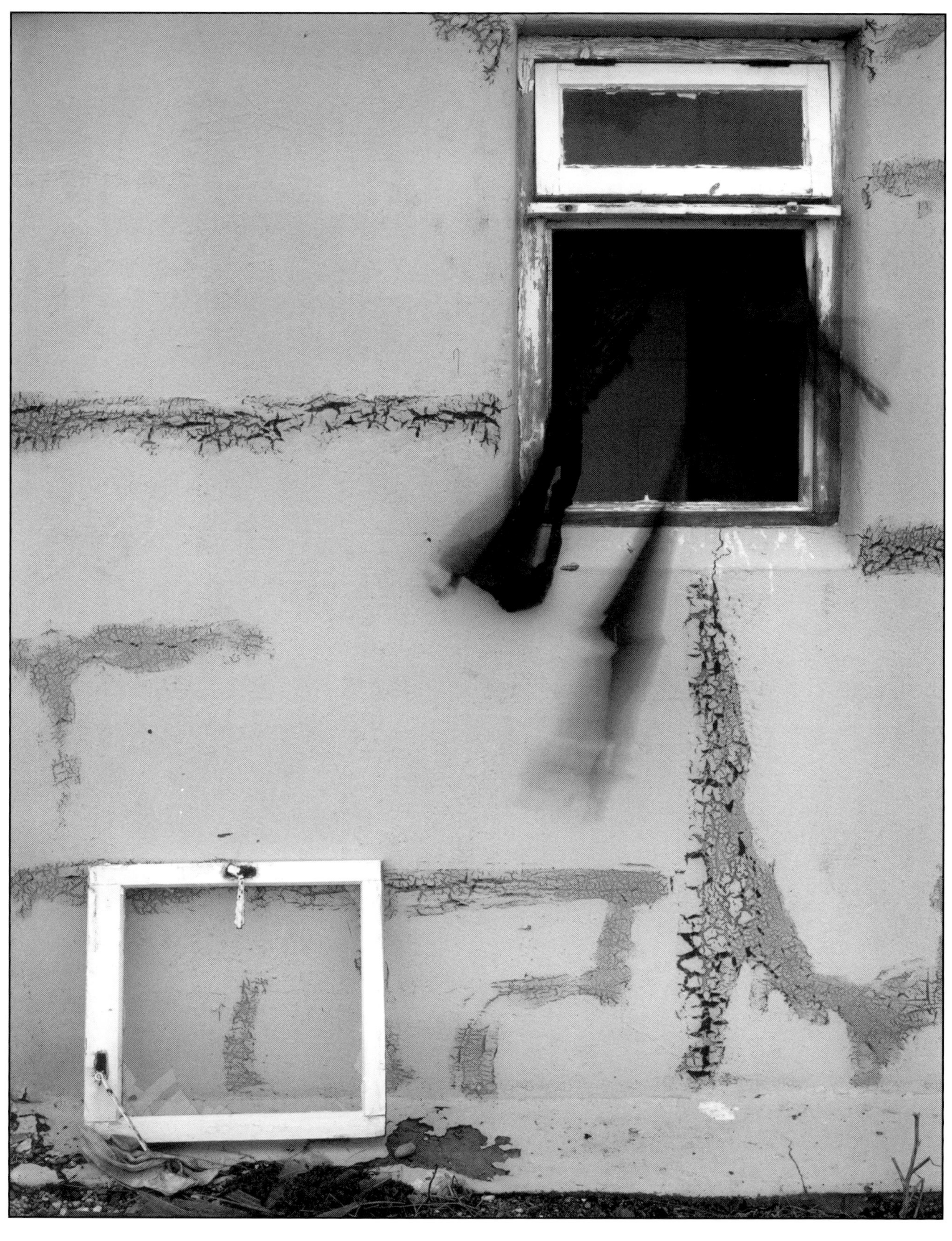

11

The breakout – from the 'Sinister window' series

Dungeness, 1994

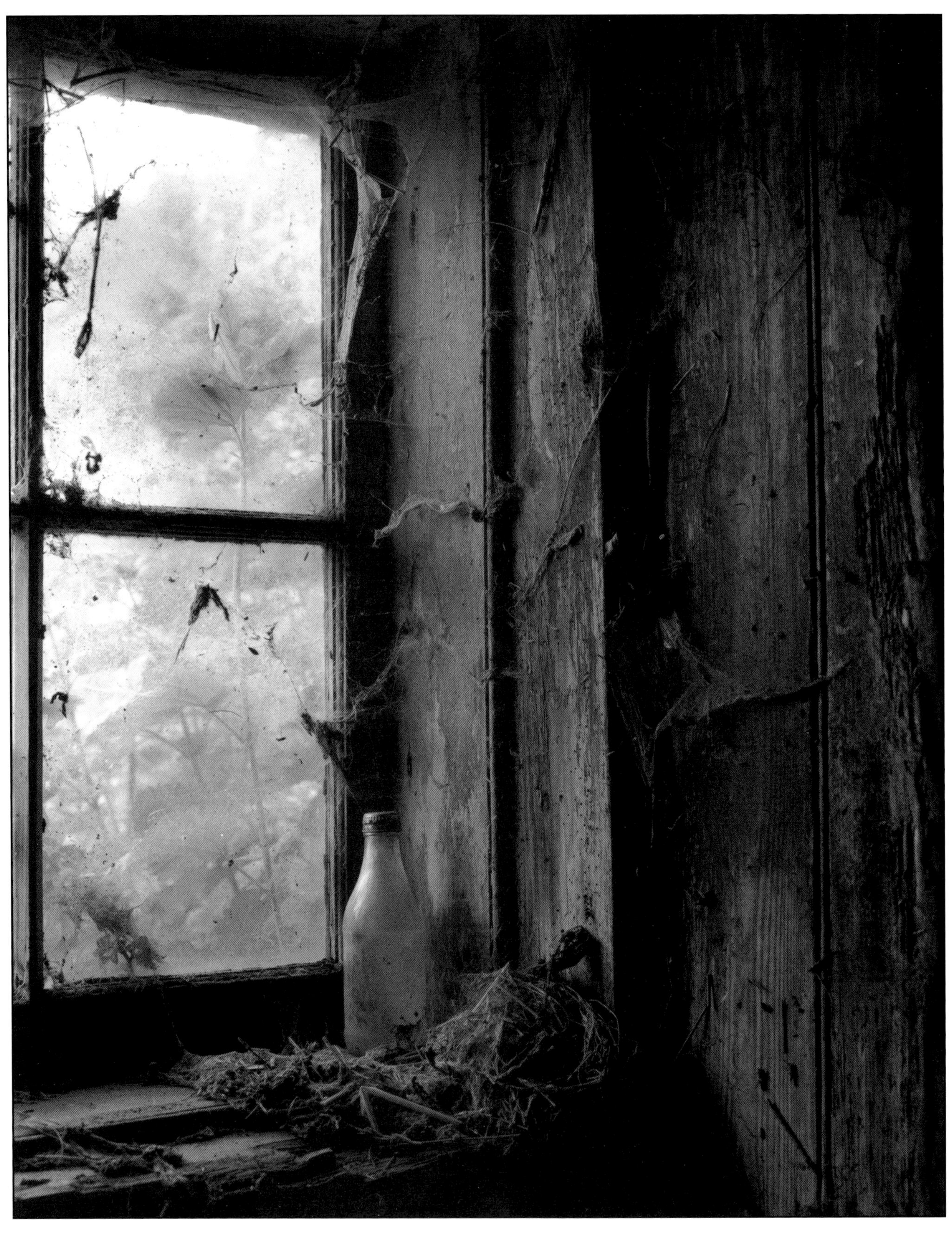

12
Neglected corner
Derelict farm, Horton Kirby, 1994

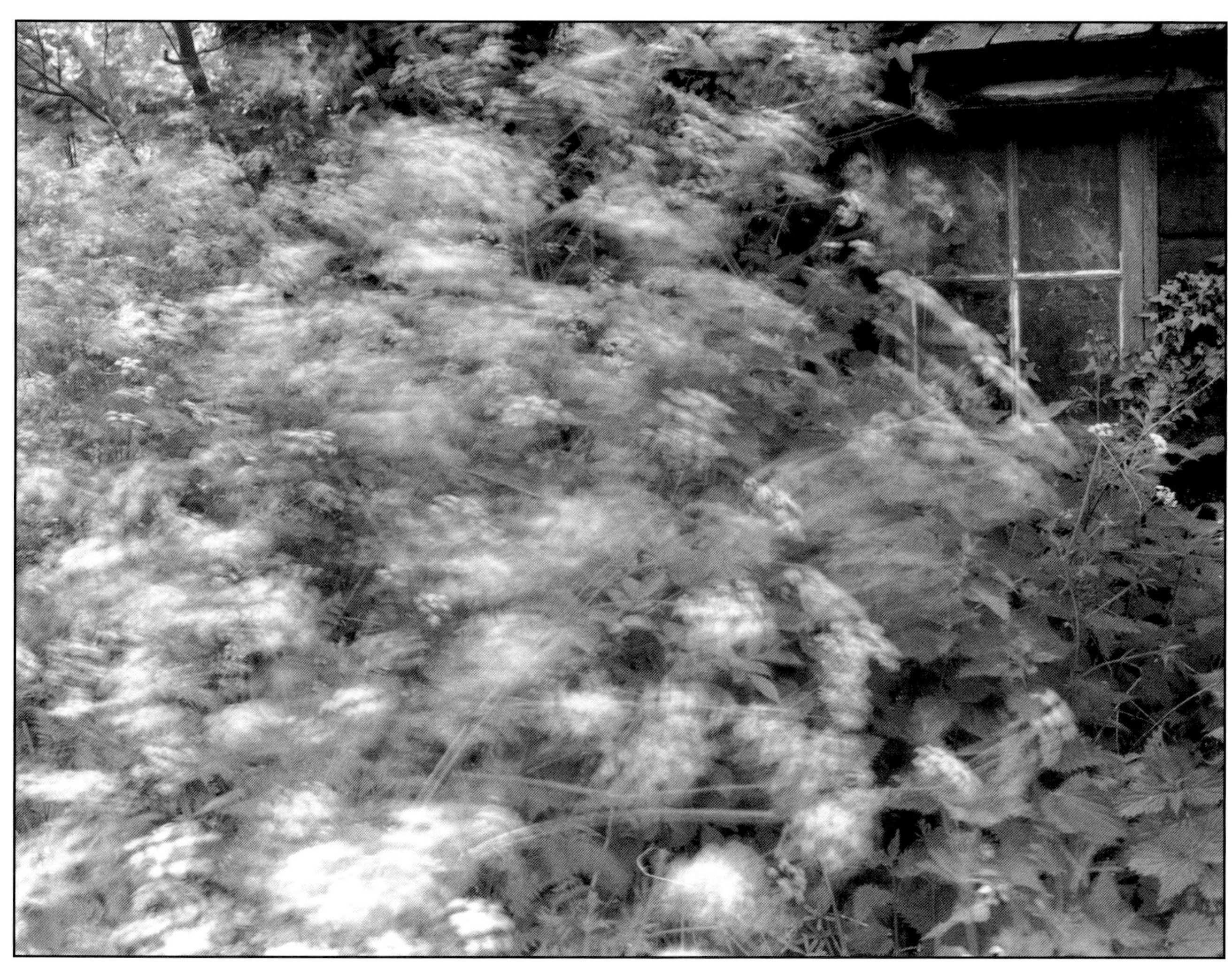

13
The disturbance – from the 'Sinister window' series
Derelict farm, Horton Kirby, 1994

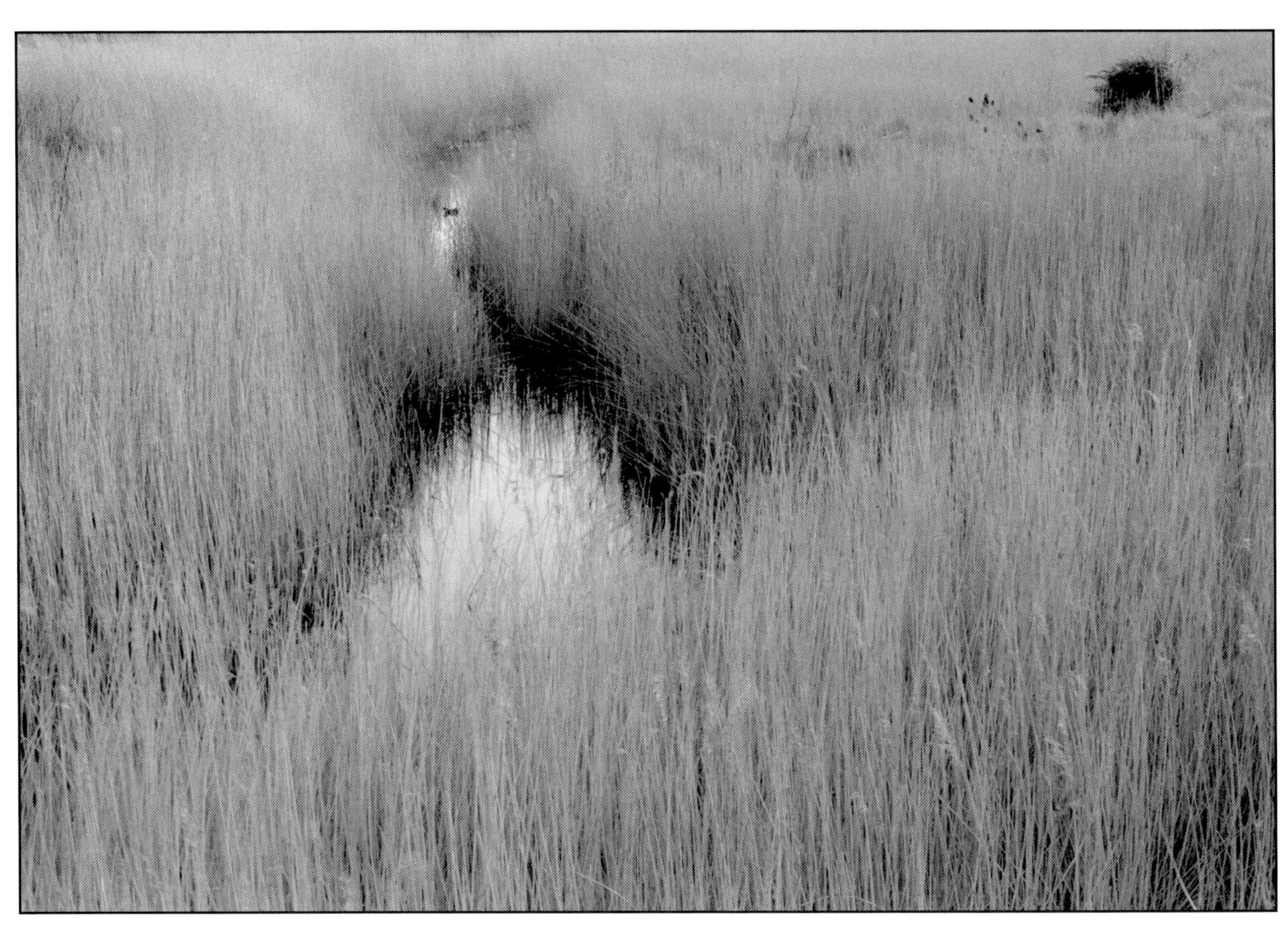

14
Wade Marshes
Minnis, 1995

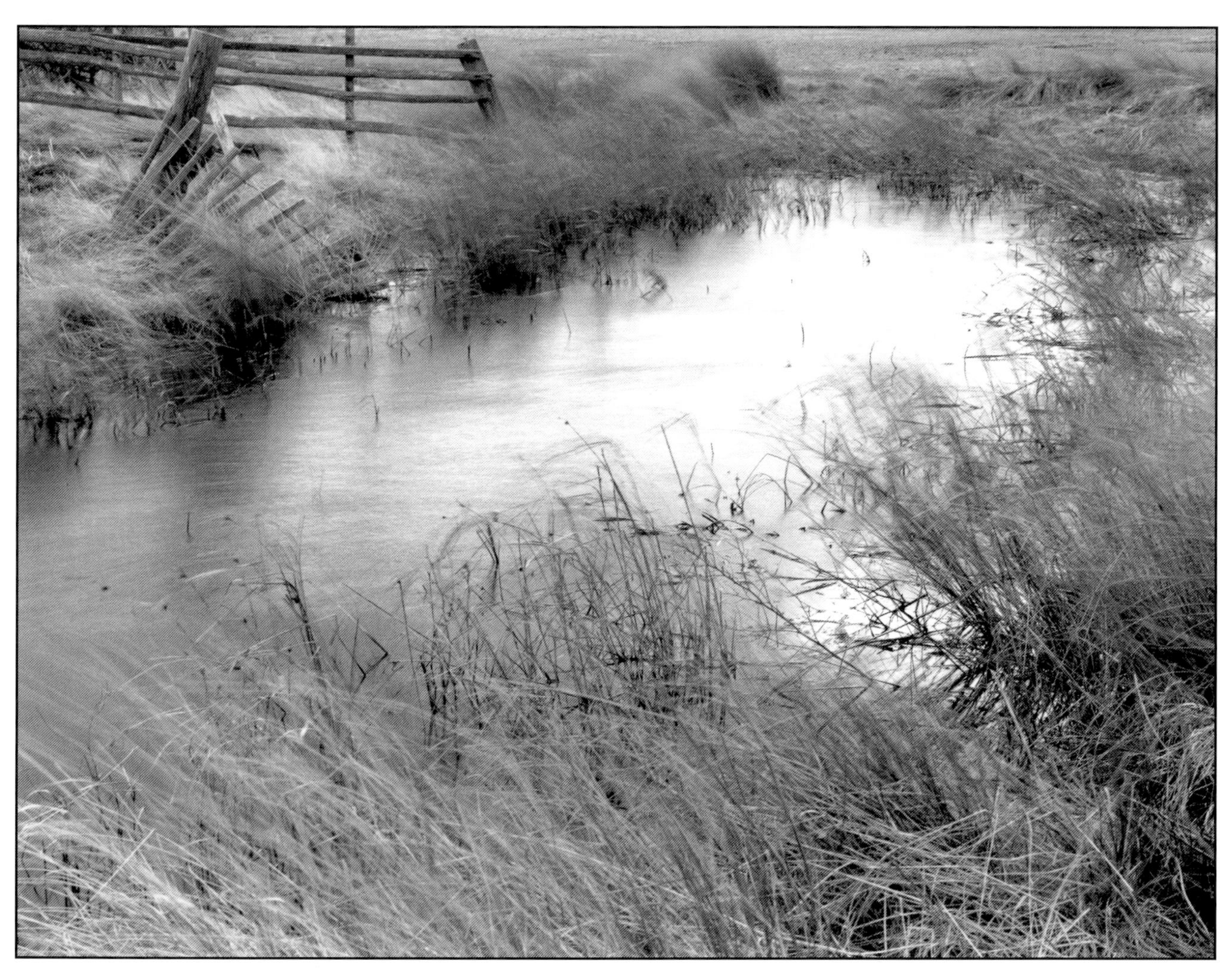

15
Windswept reeds
Cliffe Marshes, 1994

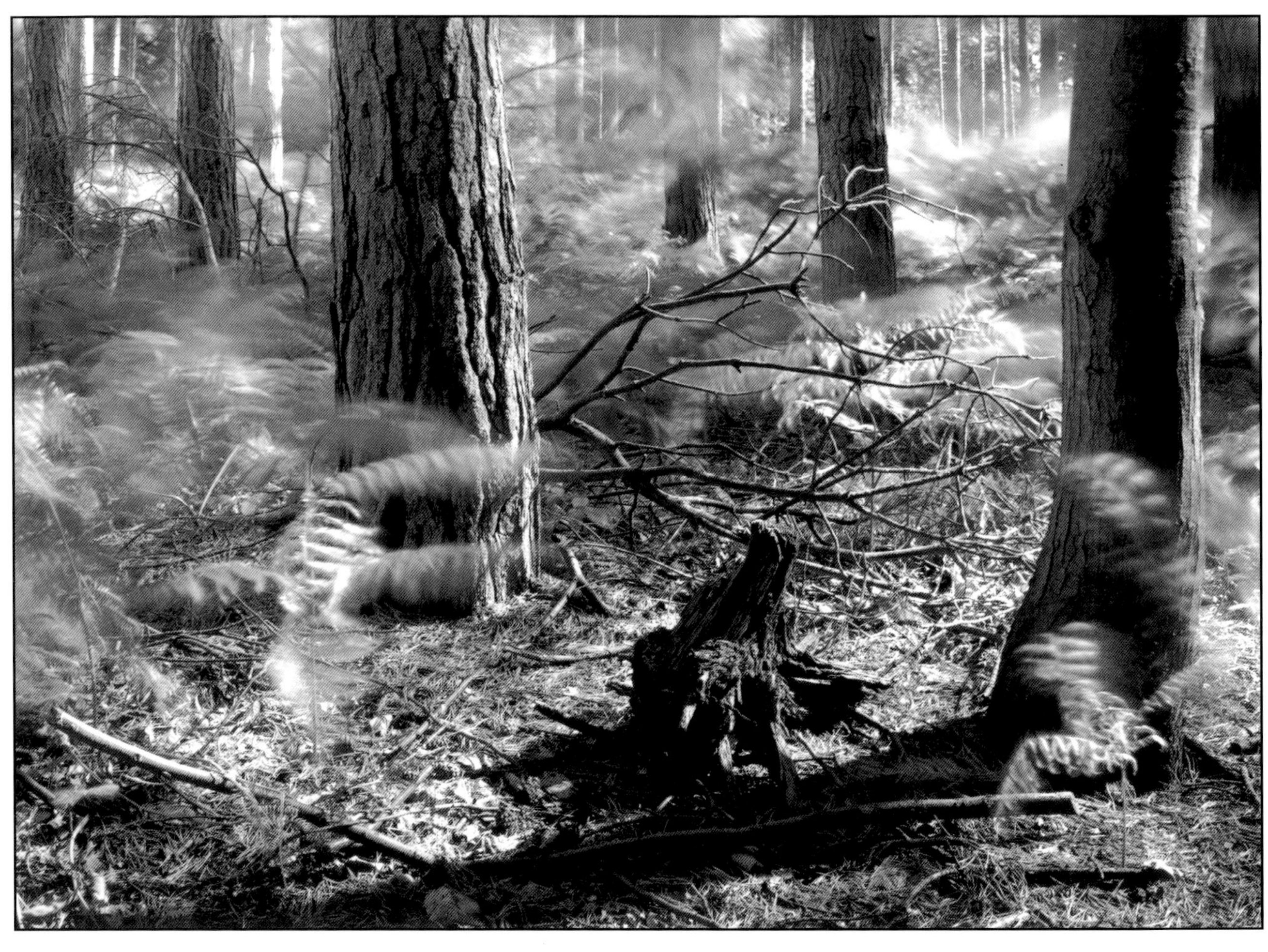

16
Pines
West Blean Wood, 1995

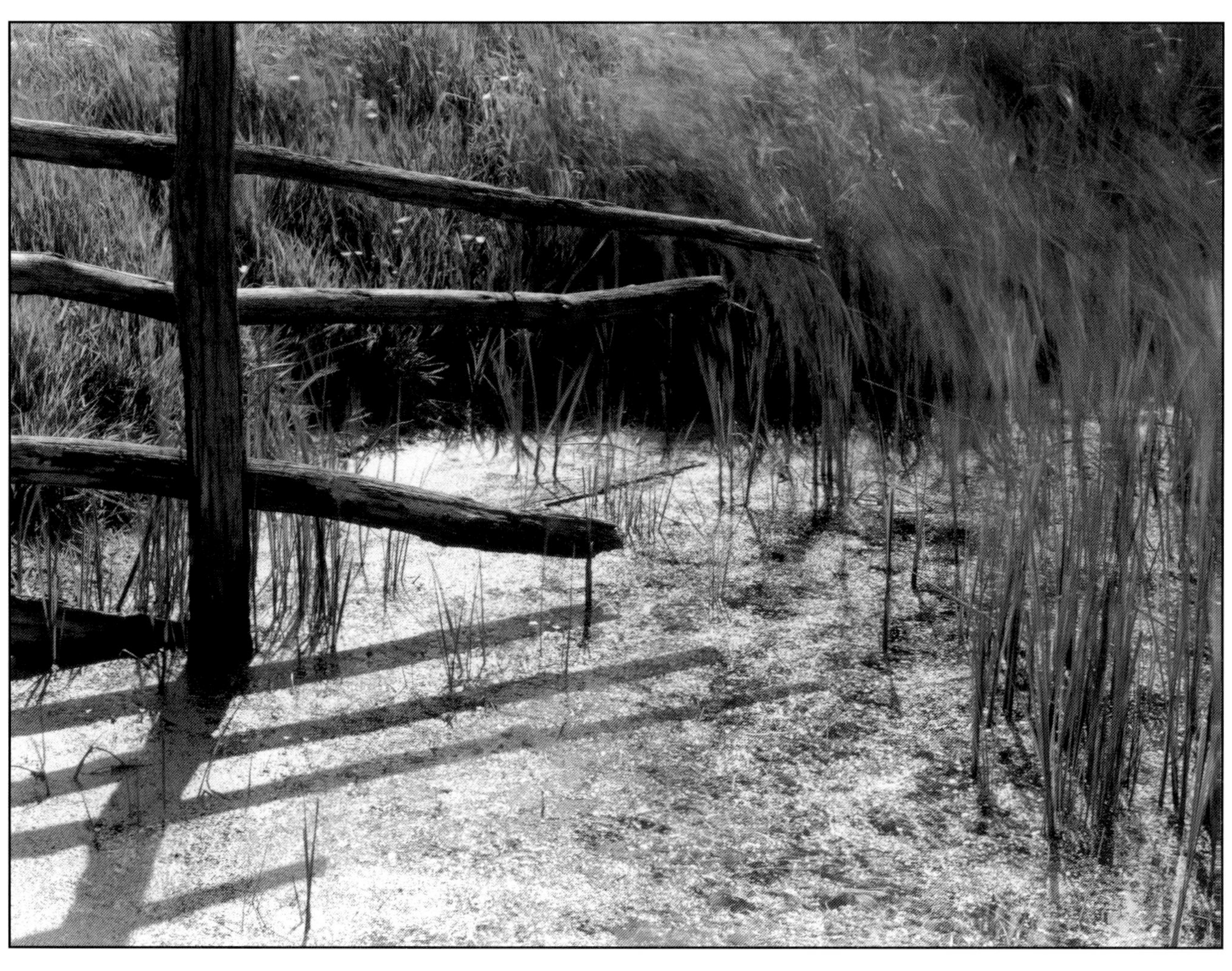

17
Fence and reeds
Cliffe Marshes, 1994

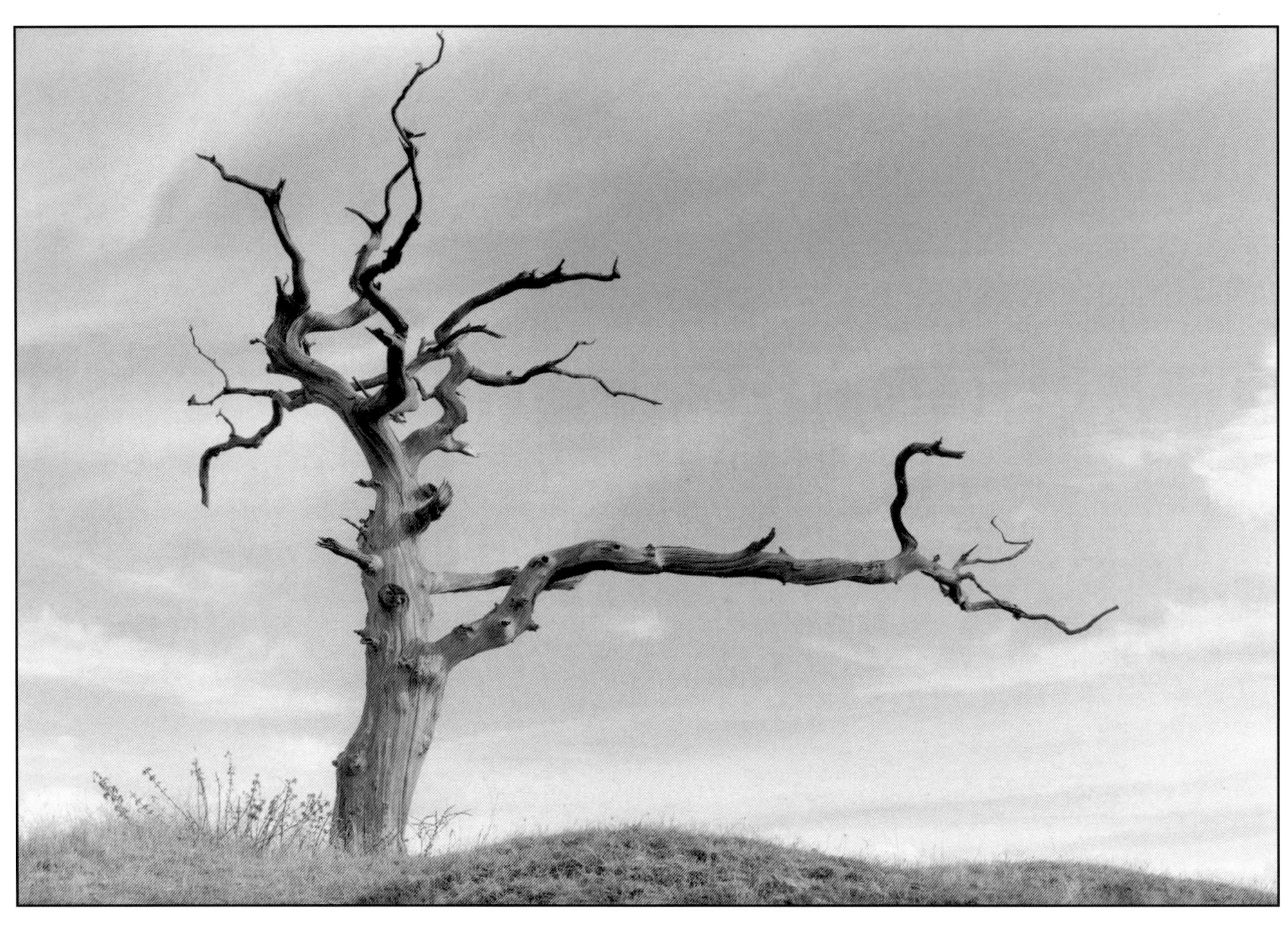

18

Dead tree

Stour Valley, 1995

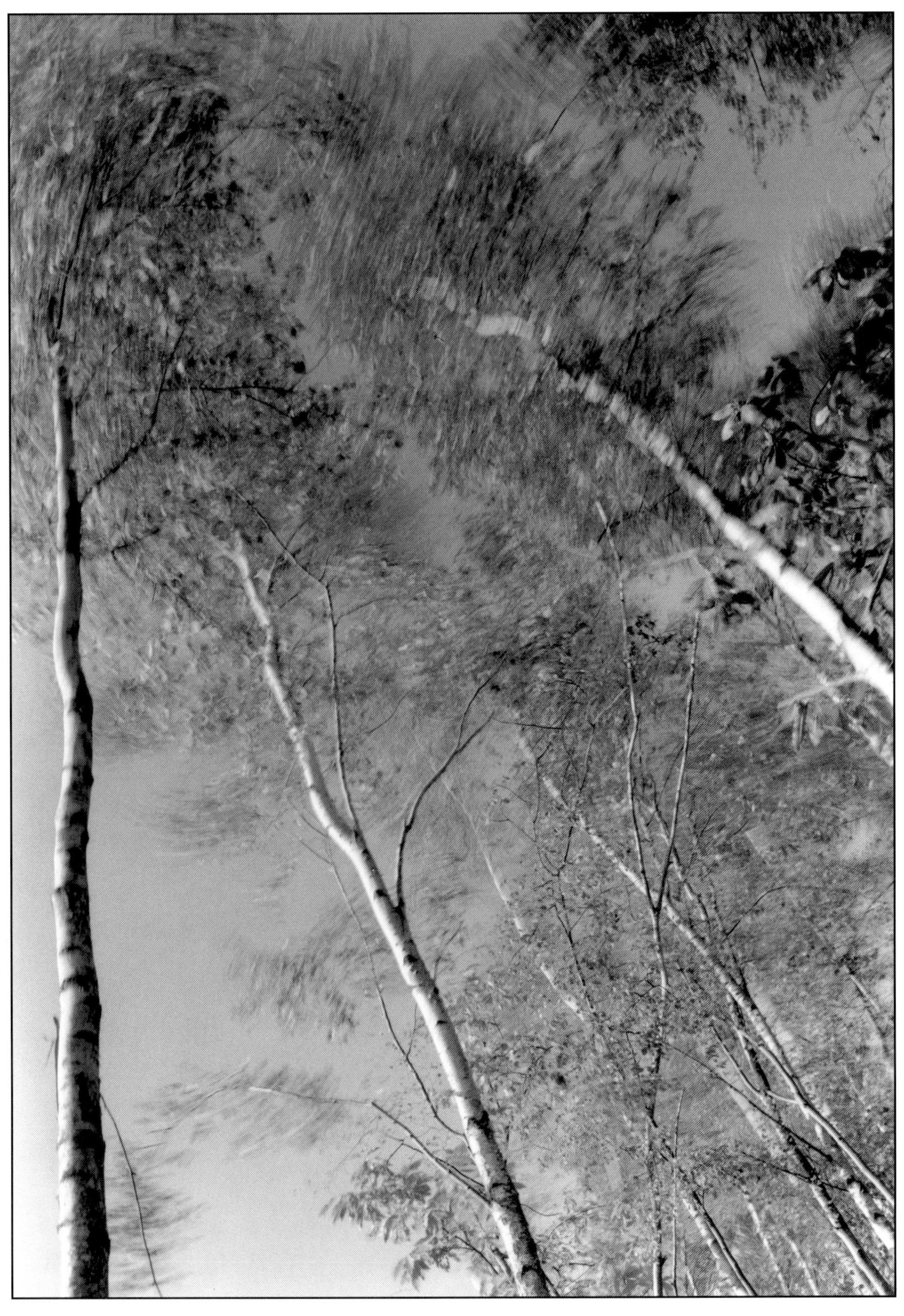

19
Dancing trees
West Blean Wood, 1995

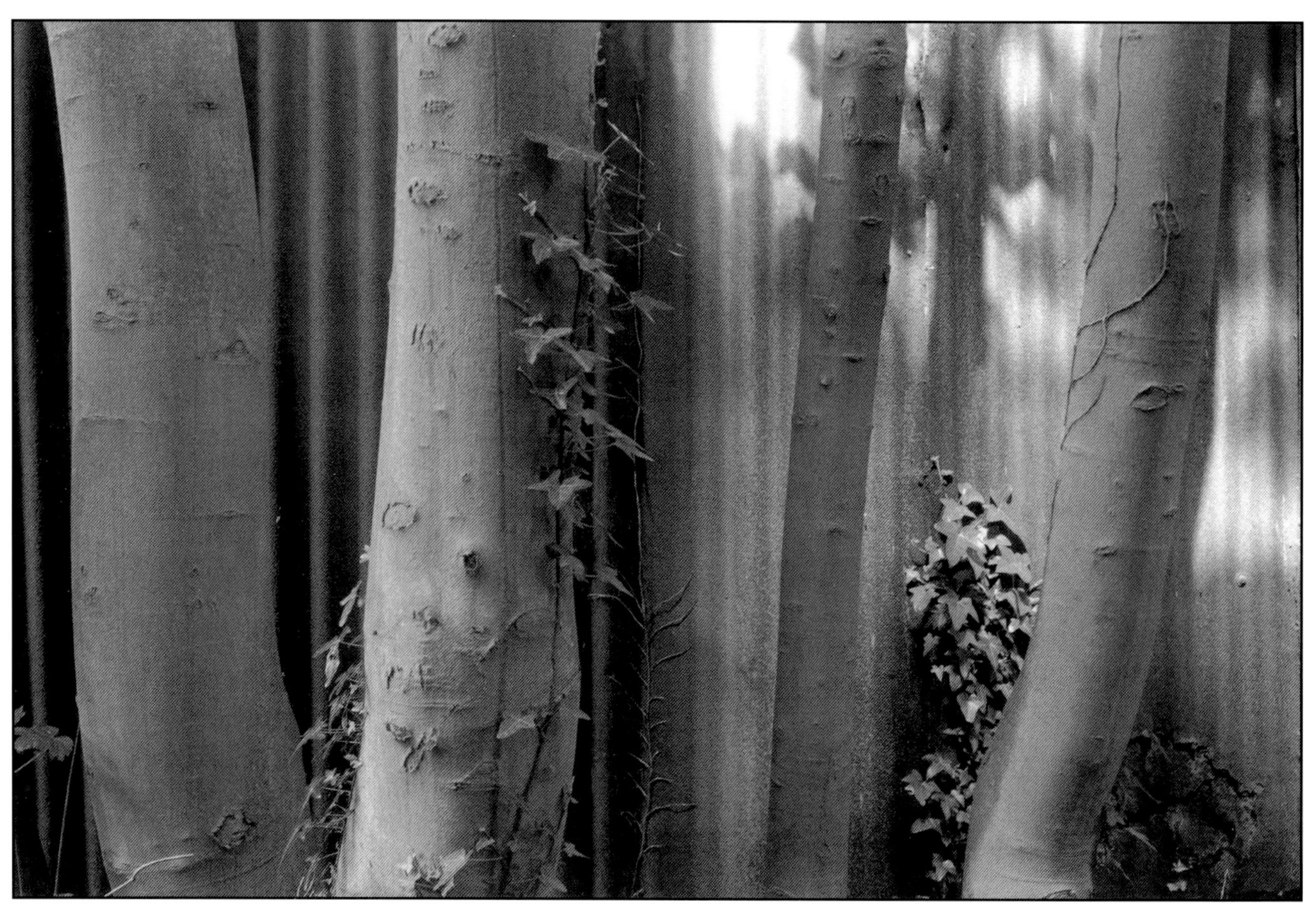

20
Trees, ivy, corrugated shed
Sandwich, 1995

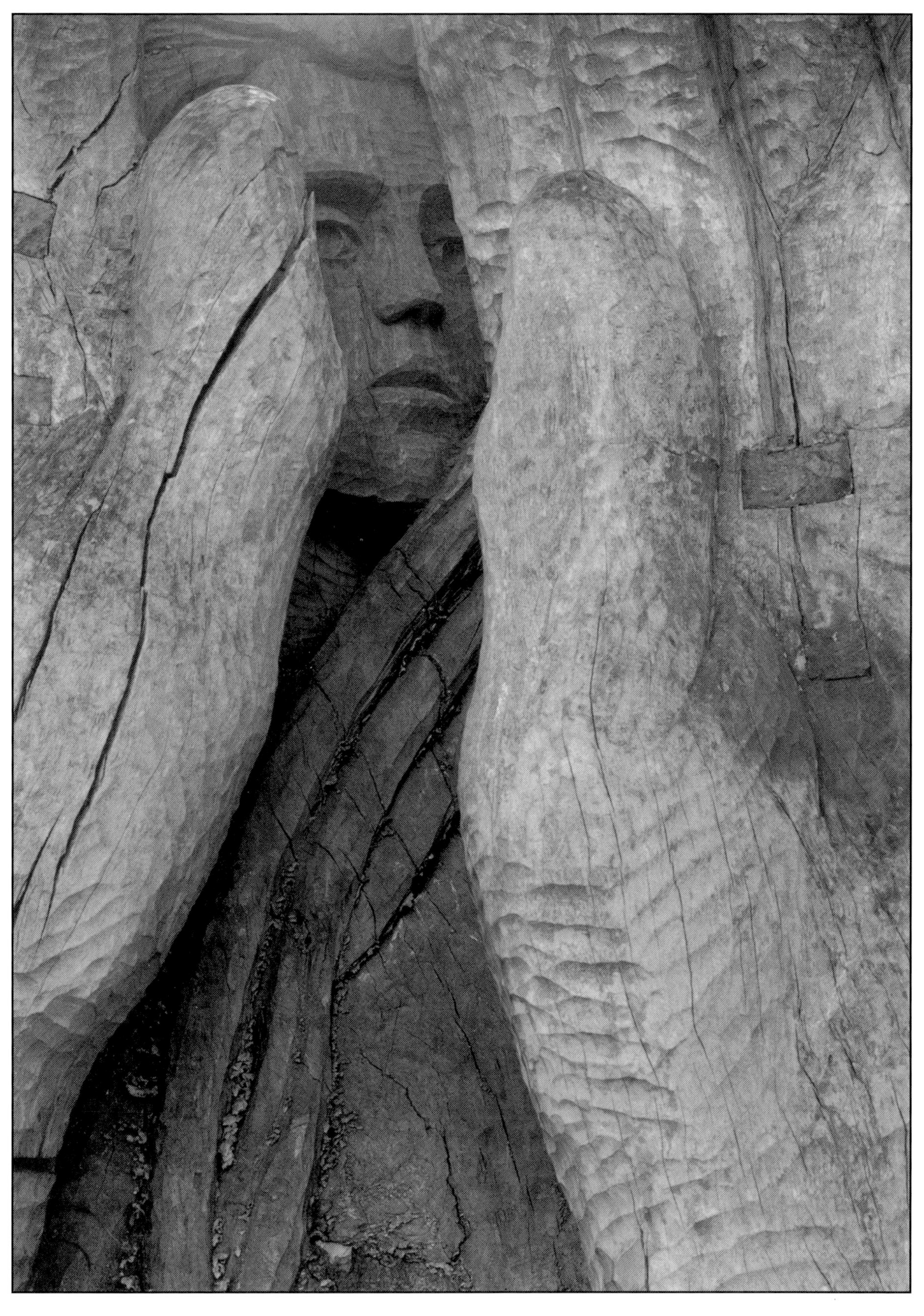

21
Tree carving
Milers Field, Canterbury, 1995

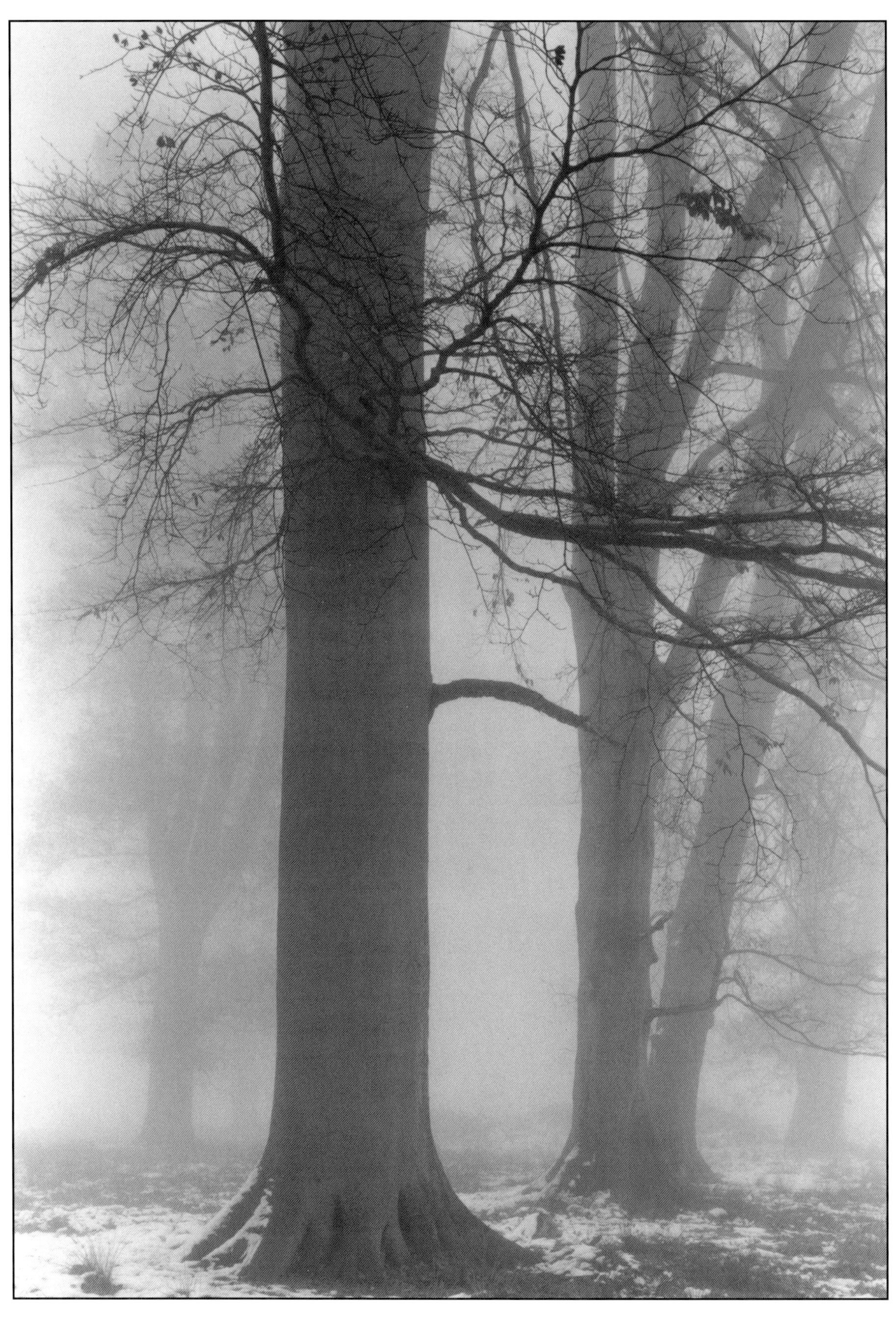

22
Trees in freezing fog
Knole Park, 1995

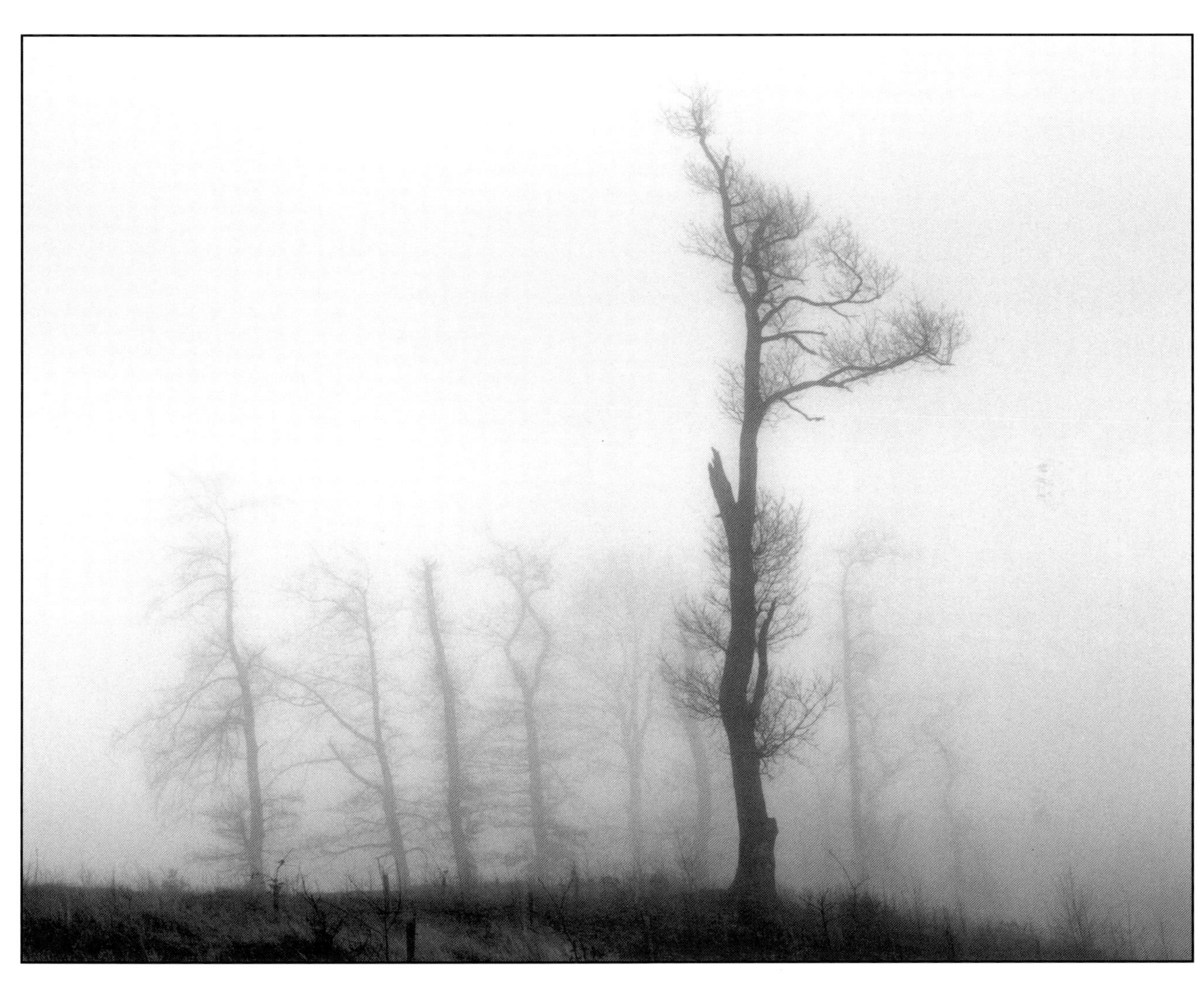

23
Trees in mist
Wrotham Hill, 1993

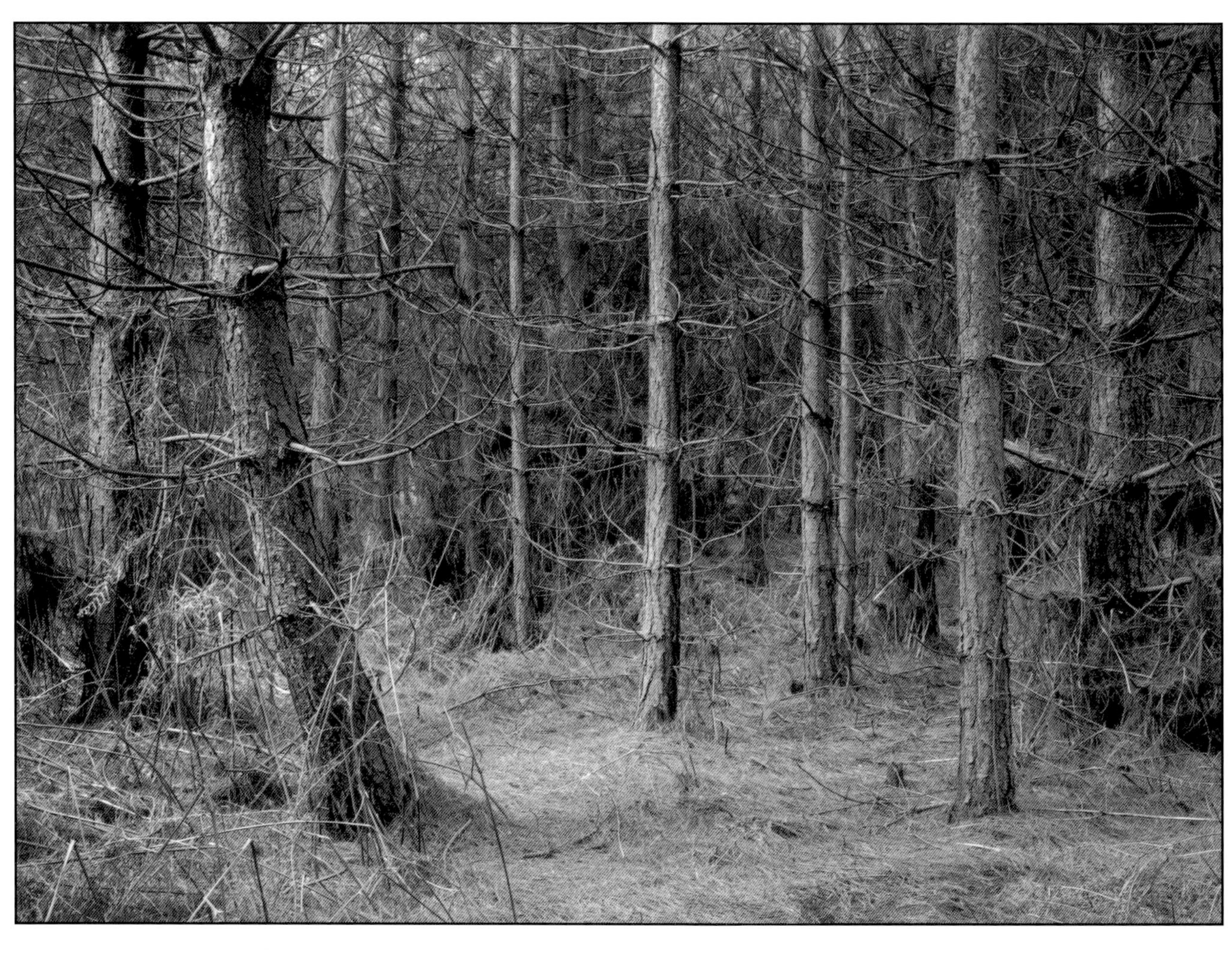

24
Pines at dusk
West Blean Wood, 1995

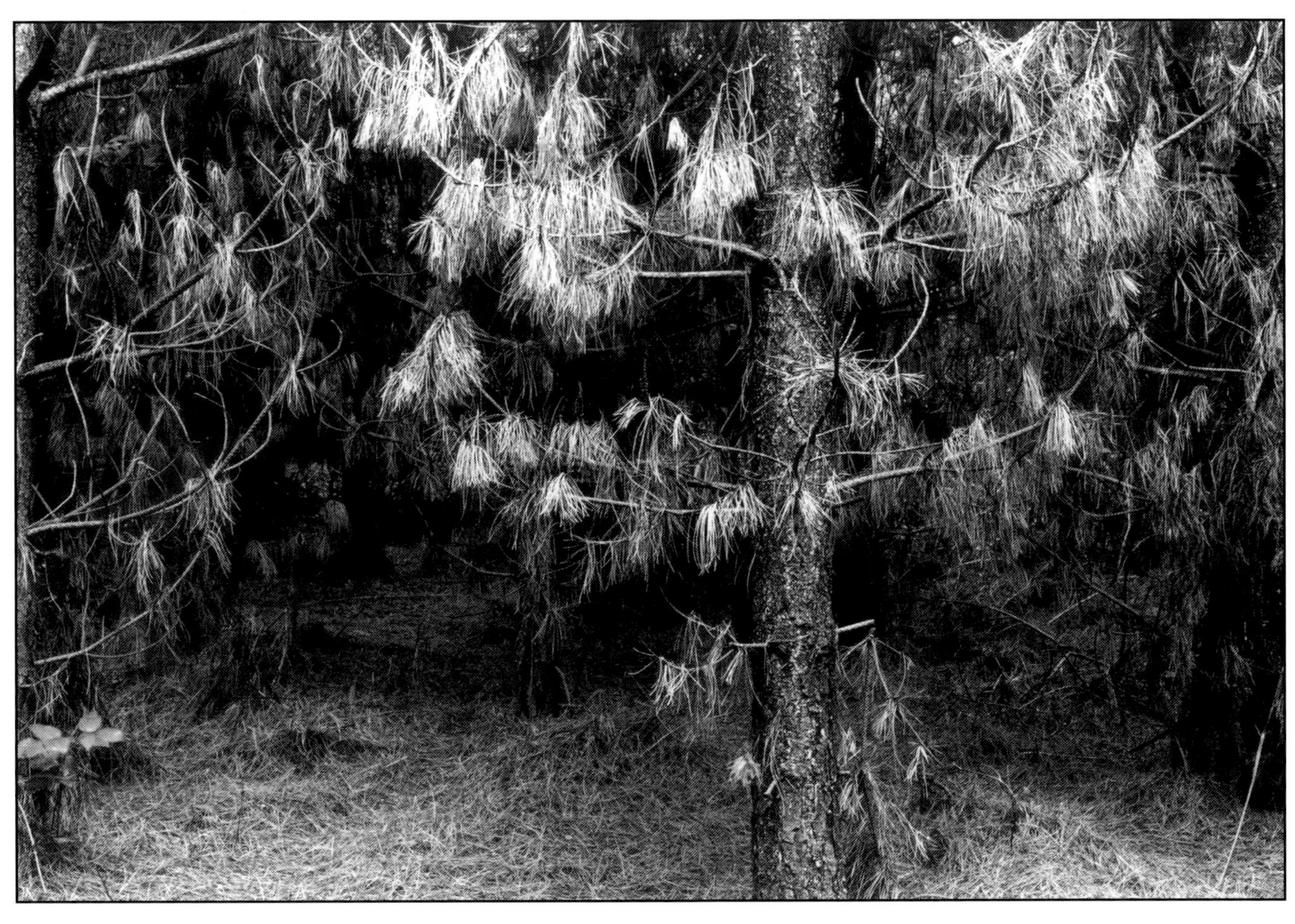

25
Pines
West Blean Wood, 1994

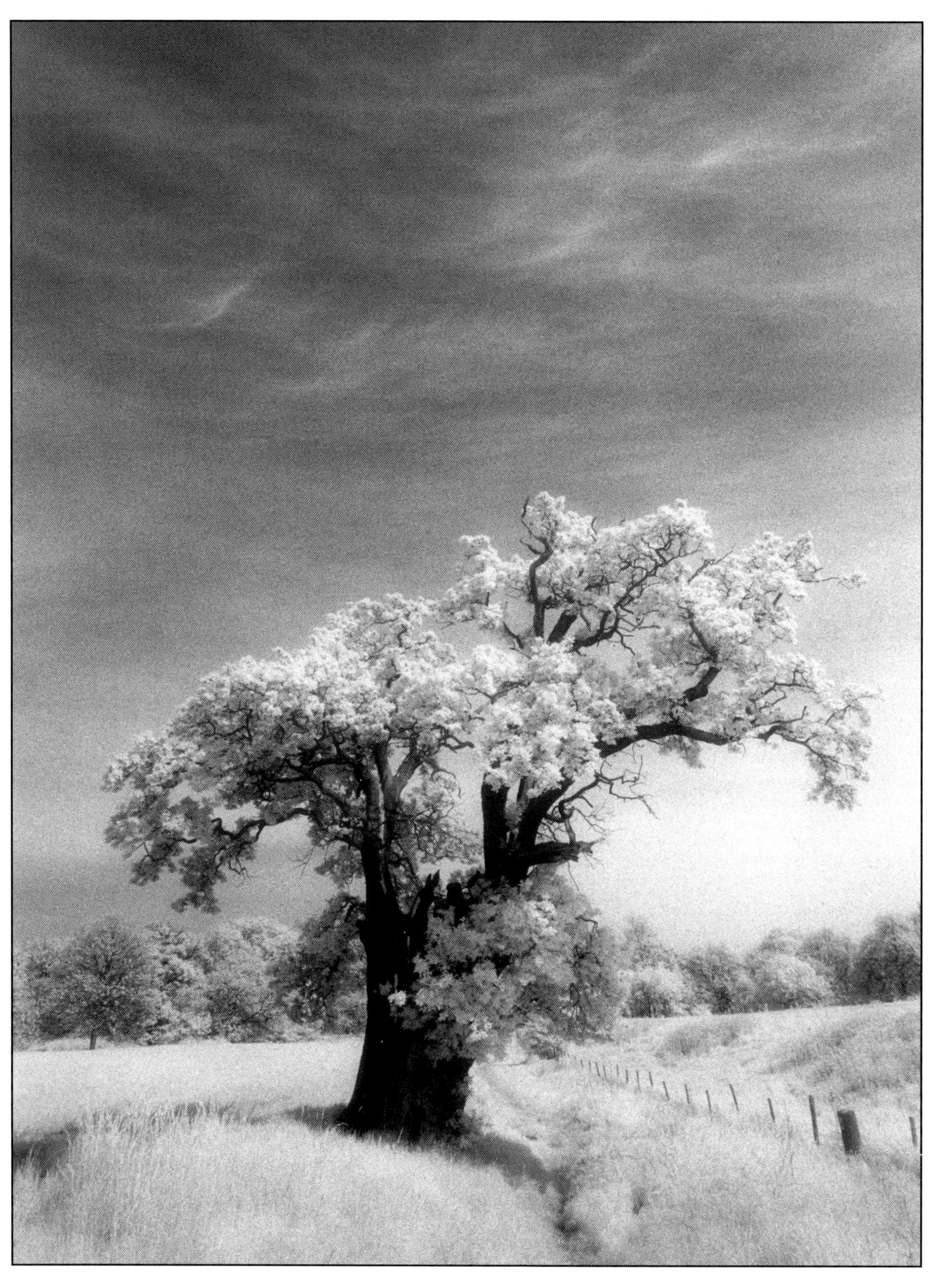

26

Gnarled oak

Near Cobham, 1983

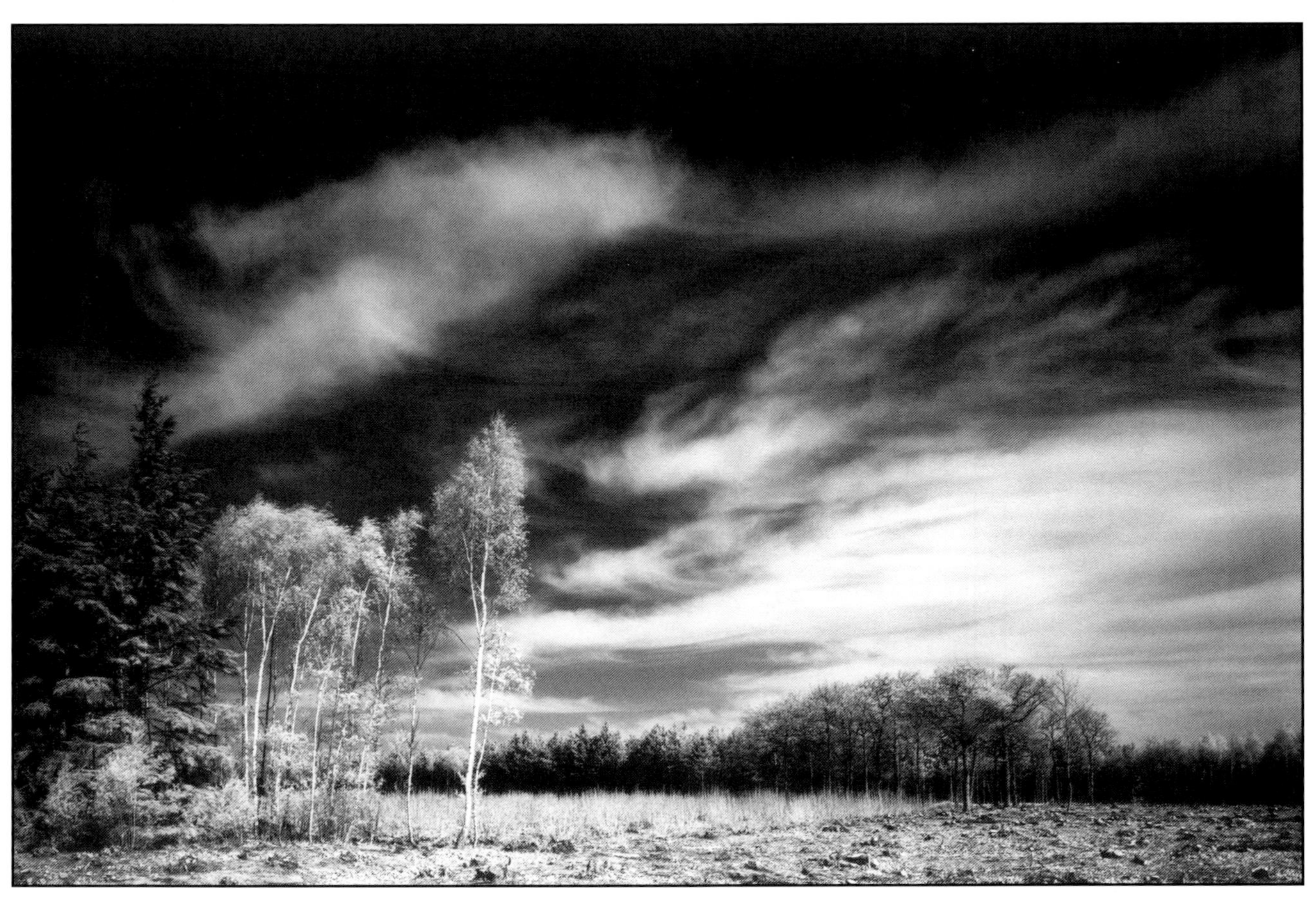

27
The clearing
West Blean Wood, 1995

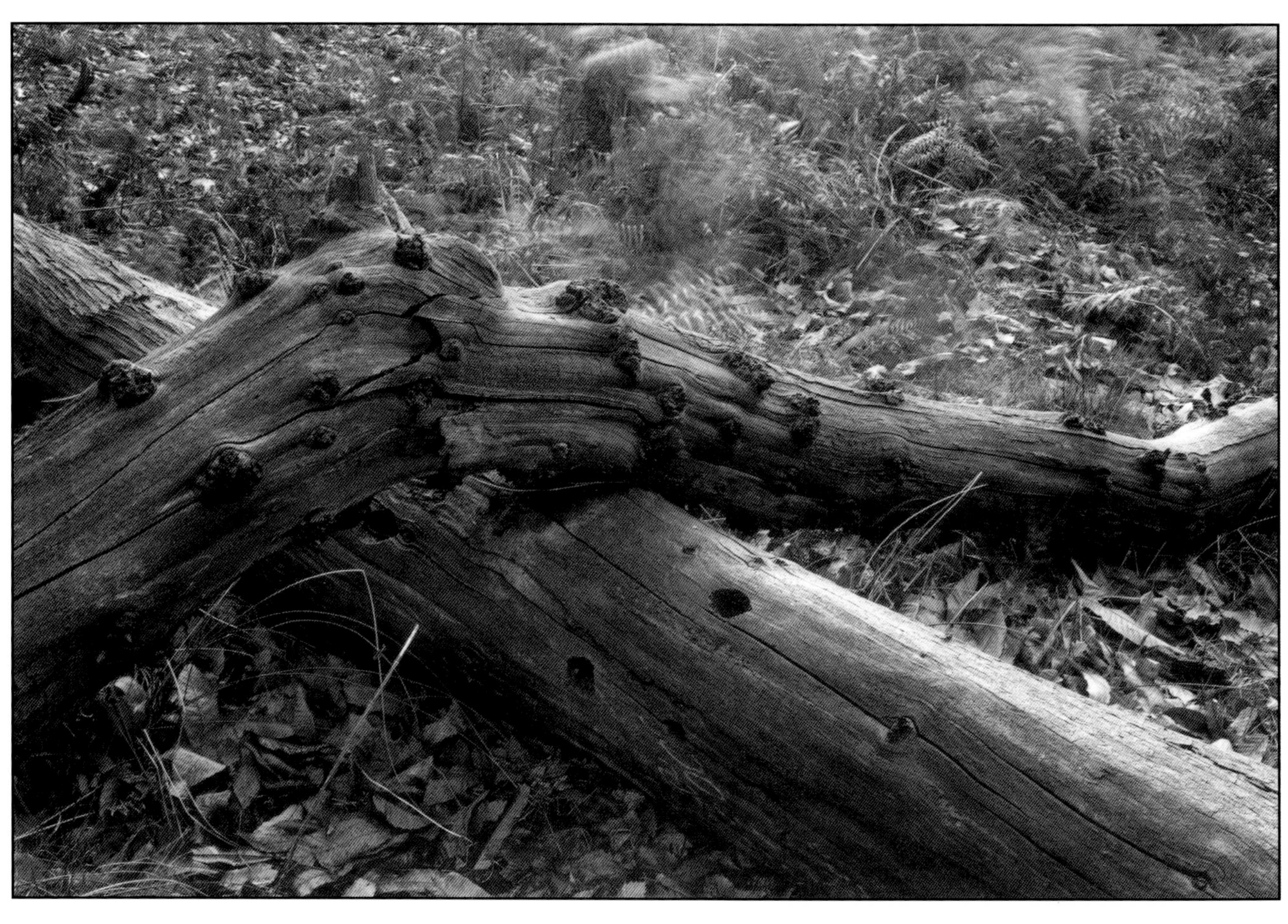

28
The fallen companions – from the 'Broken dreams' series
Knole Park, 1994

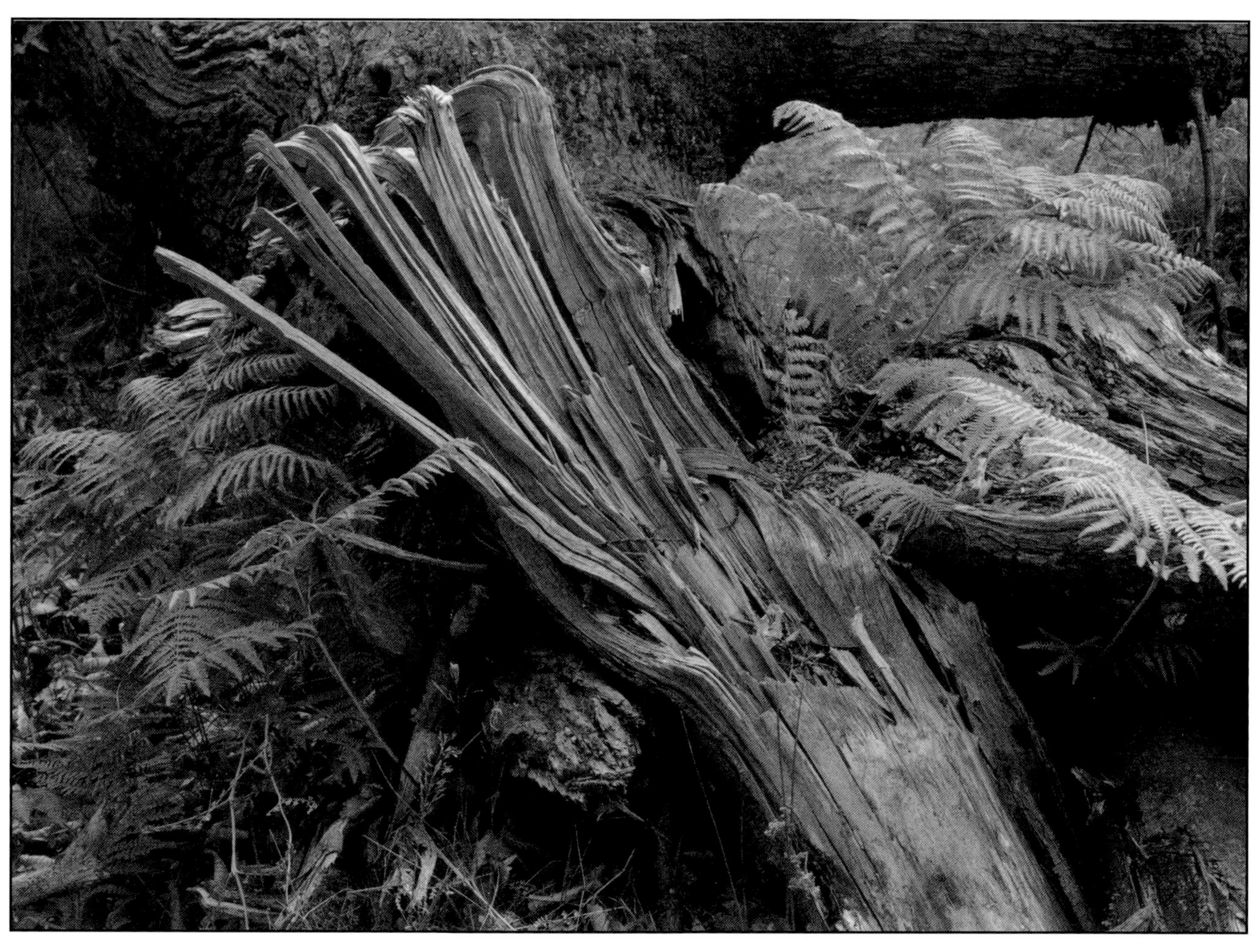

29
The clawed hand
Knole Park, 1995

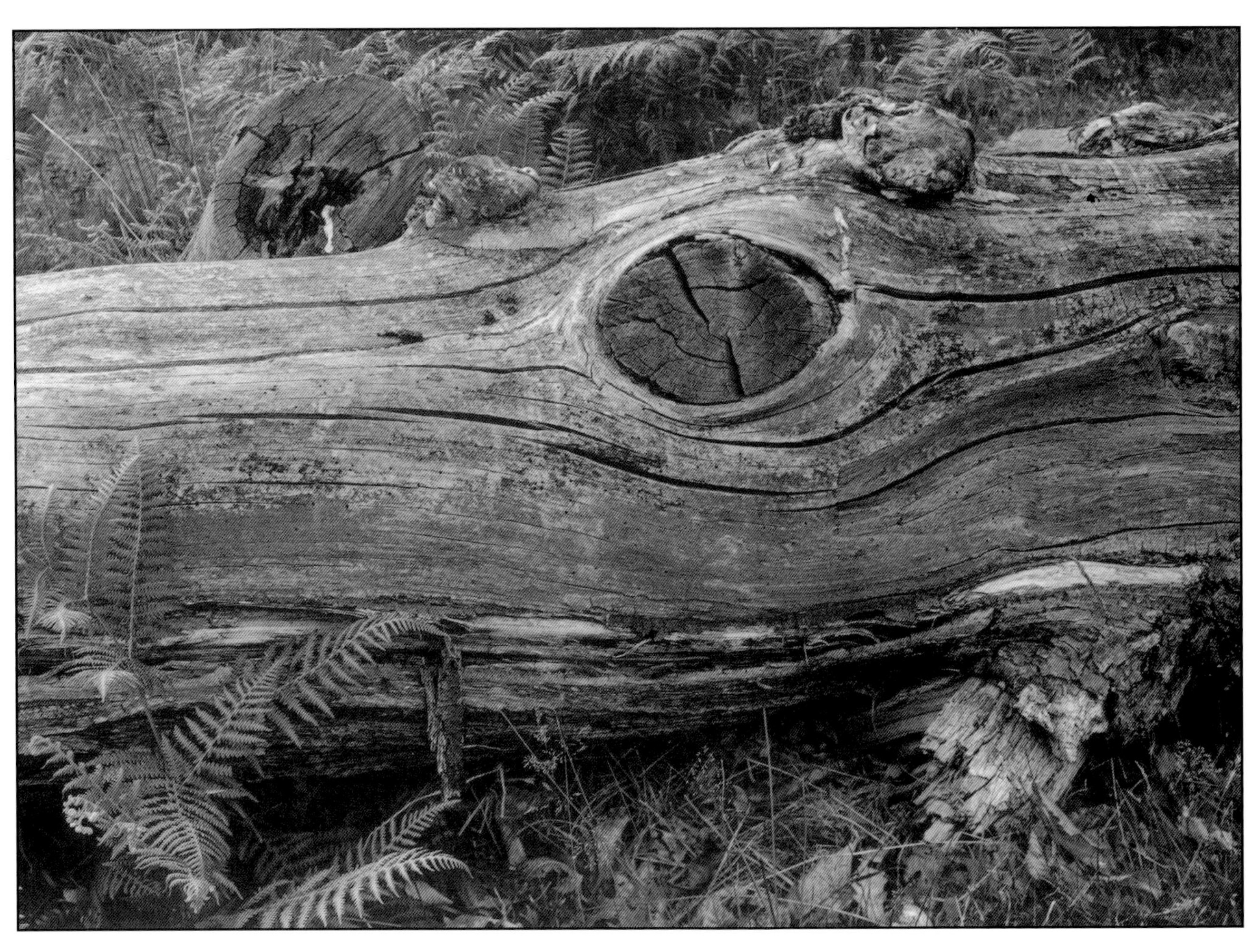

30
Lying in wait
Knole Park, 1995

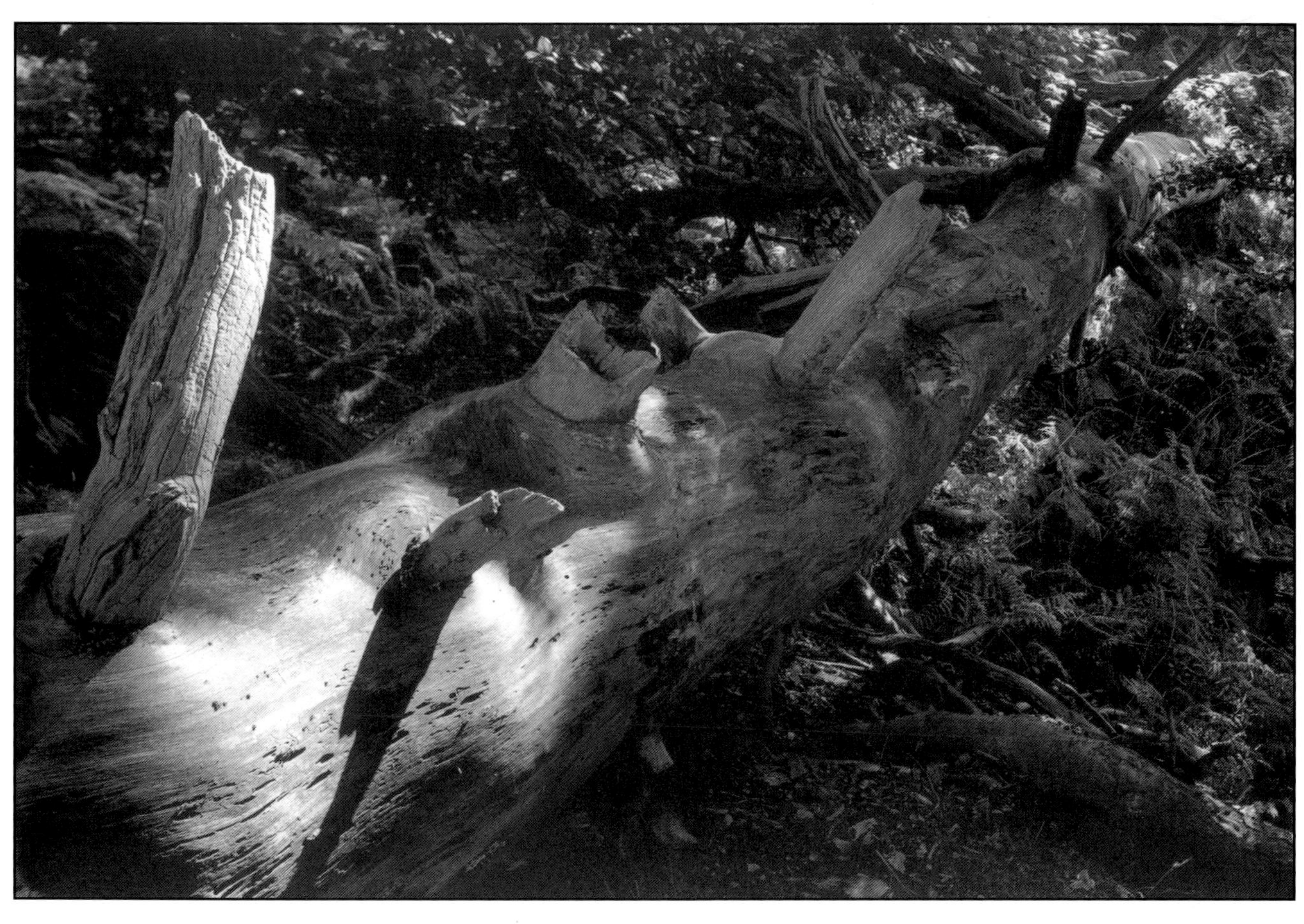

31
Fallen tree
Knole Park, 1995

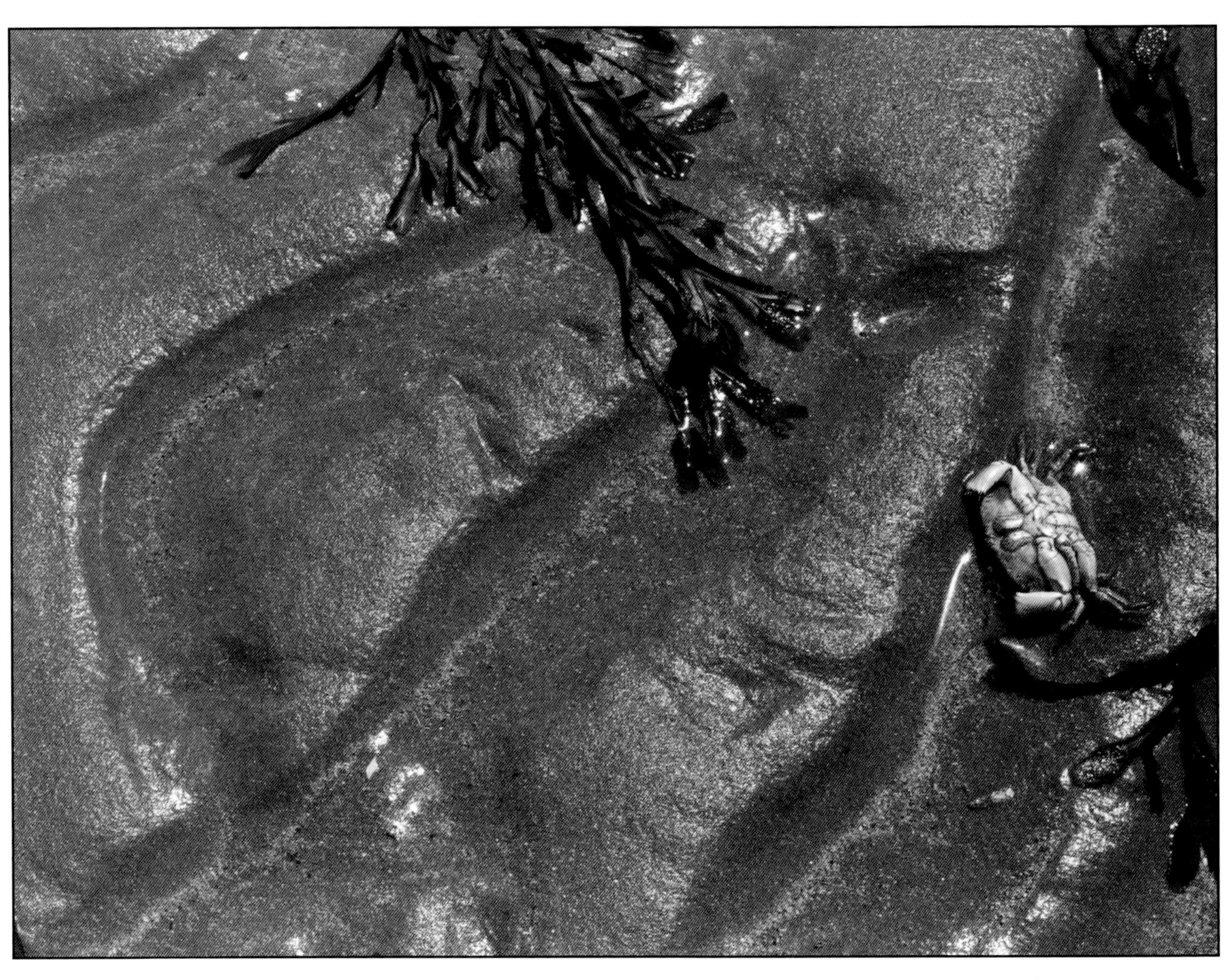

32

Turn of the tide – from the 'Broken Dreams' series

Cliftonville, Margate, 1994

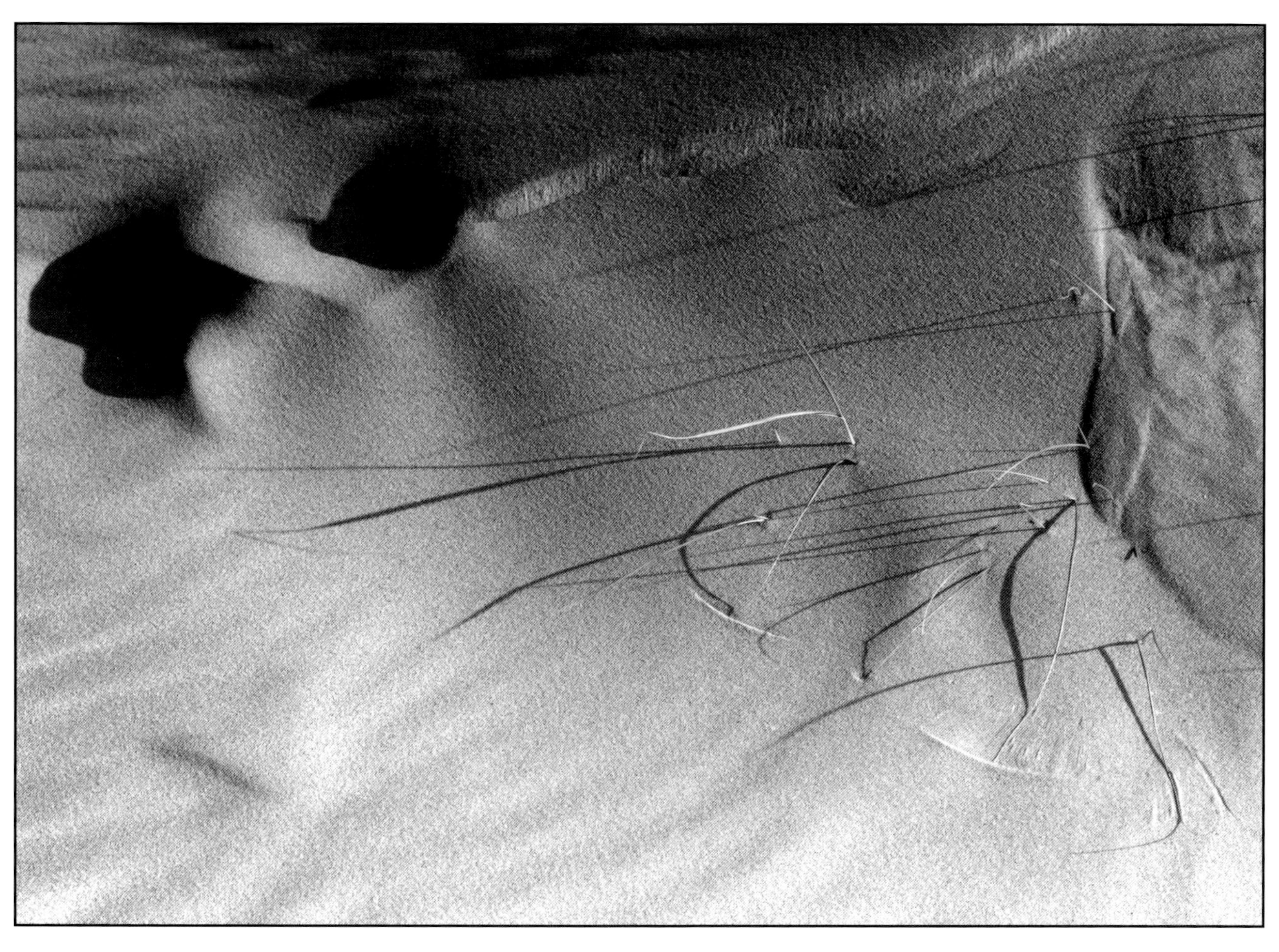

33
Sand and grasses
Greatstone-on-Sea, 1992

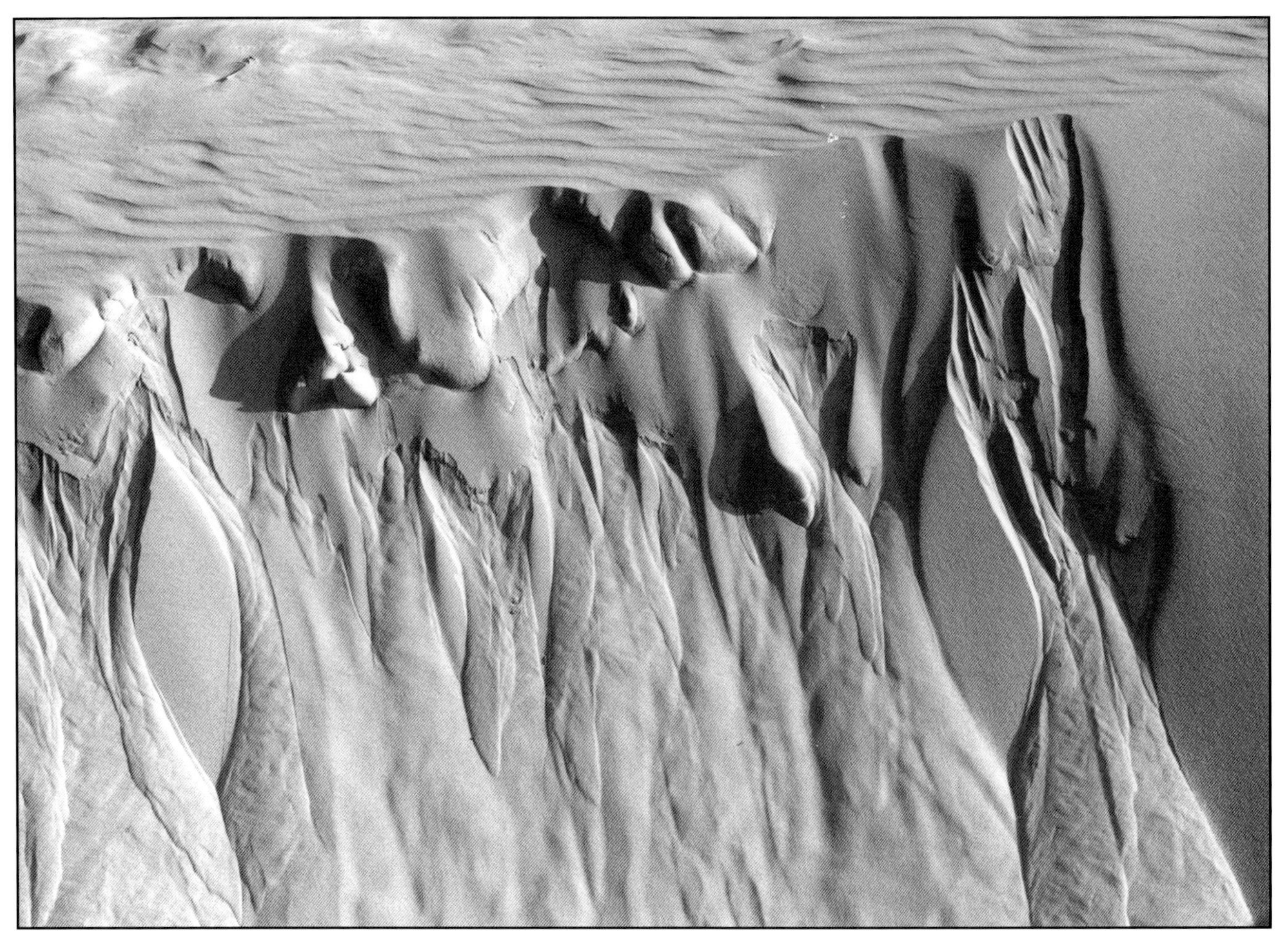

34
Sand form 1
Greatstone-on-Sea, 1992

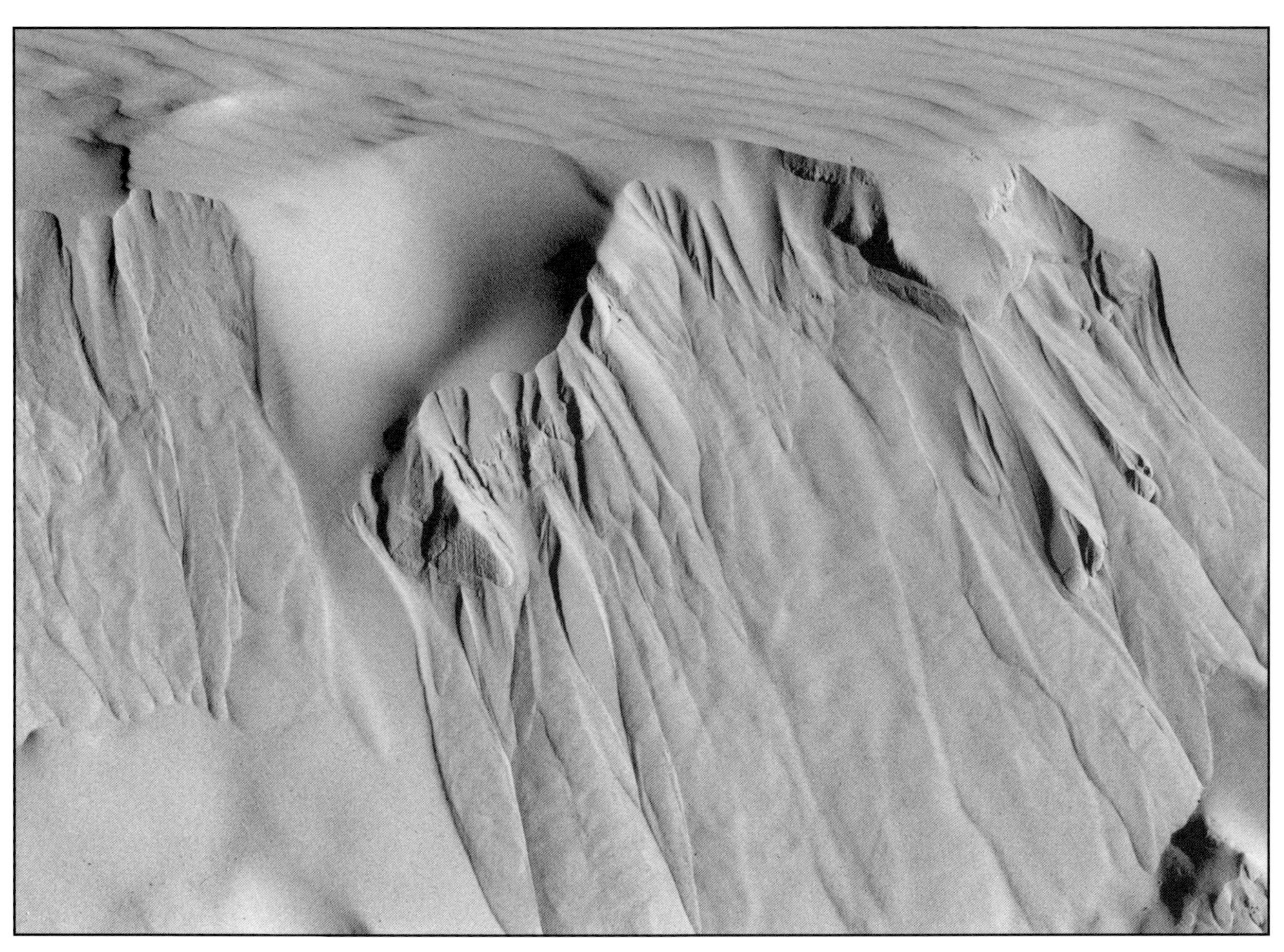

35
Sand form 2
Greatstone-on-Sea, 1992

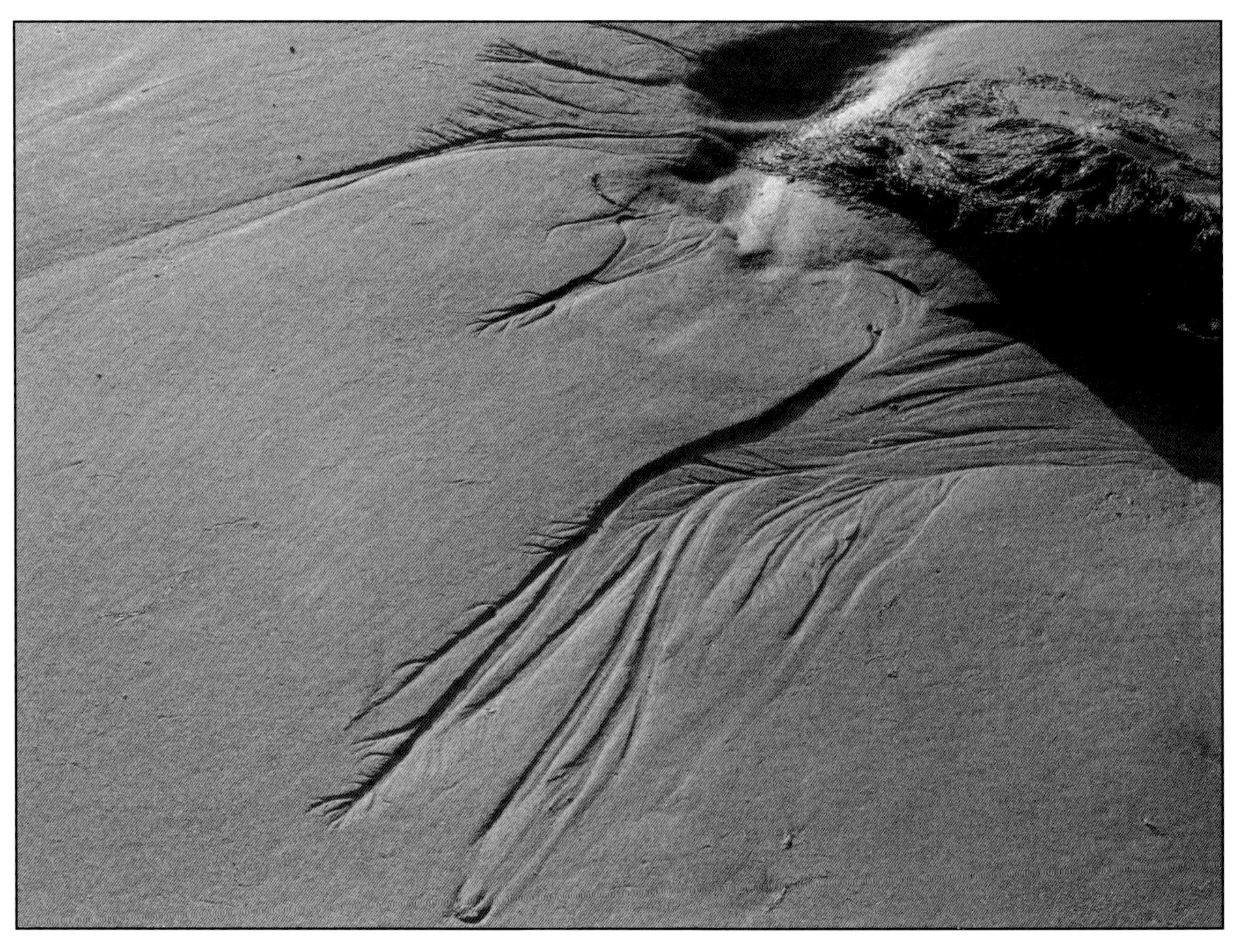

36
Beach detail
Beltinge, 1995

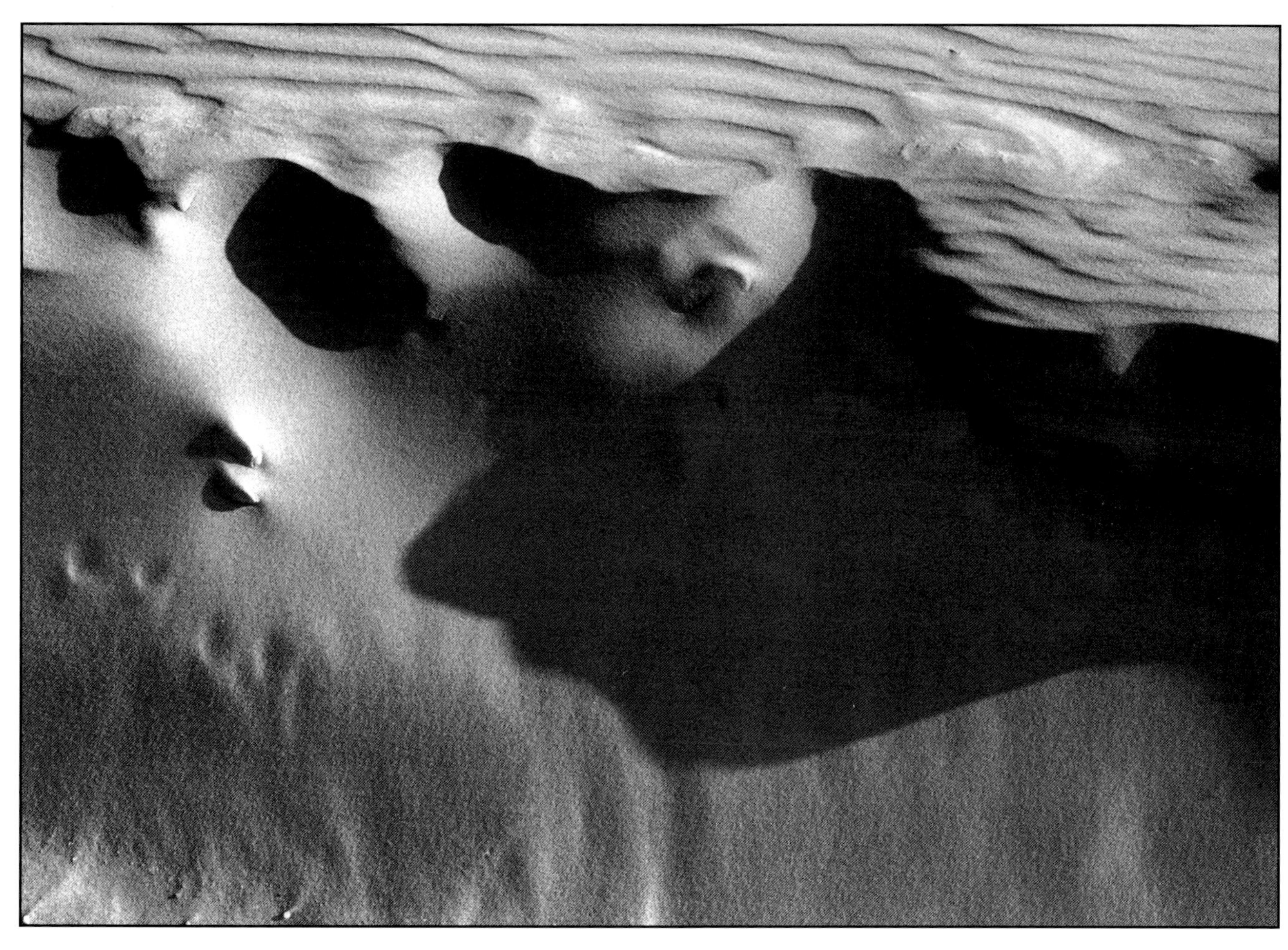

37
Sand form 3
Greatstone-on-Sea, 1995

38
Reculver from Minnis Bay
1995

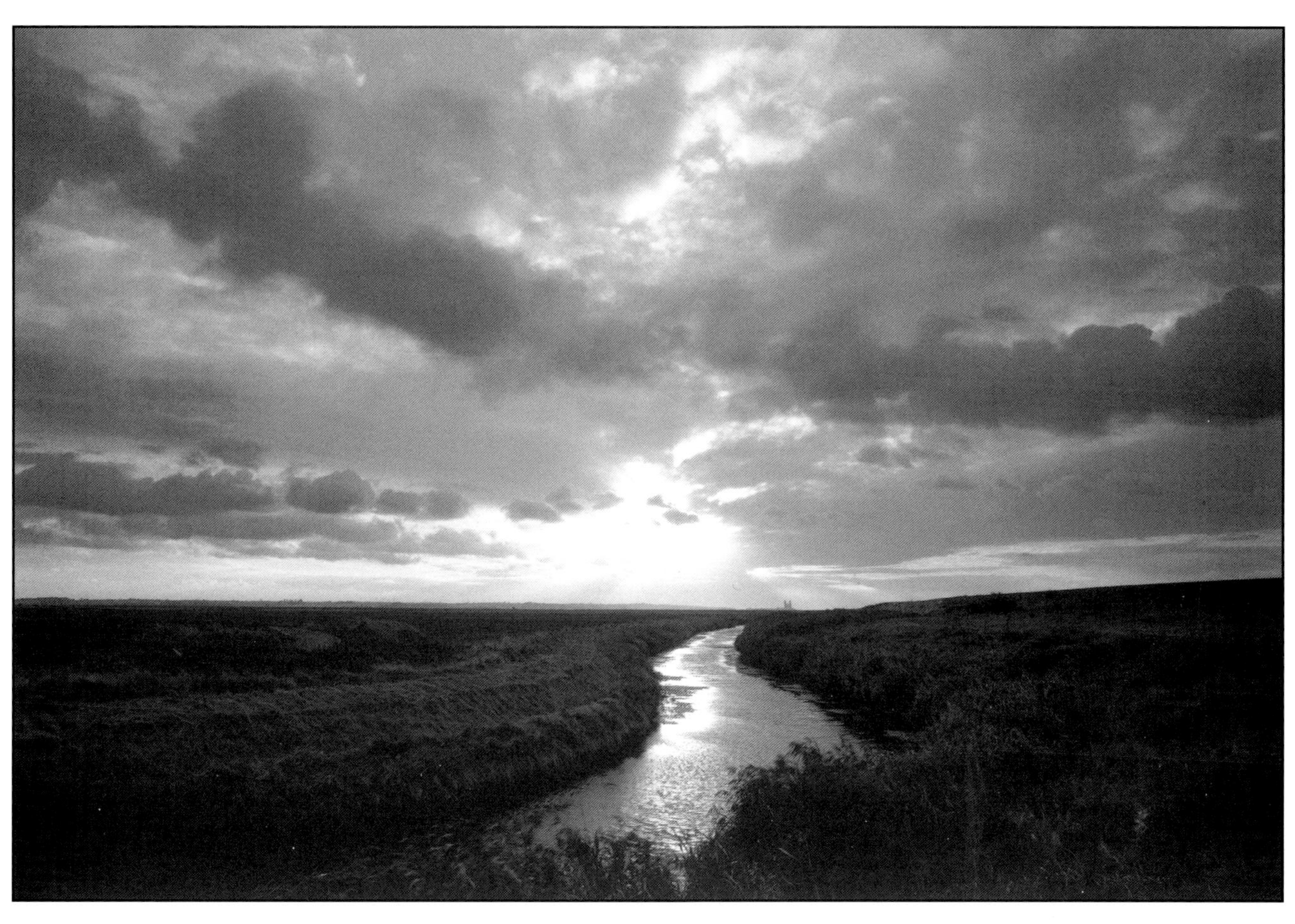

39
Reculver from Wade Marshes
1994

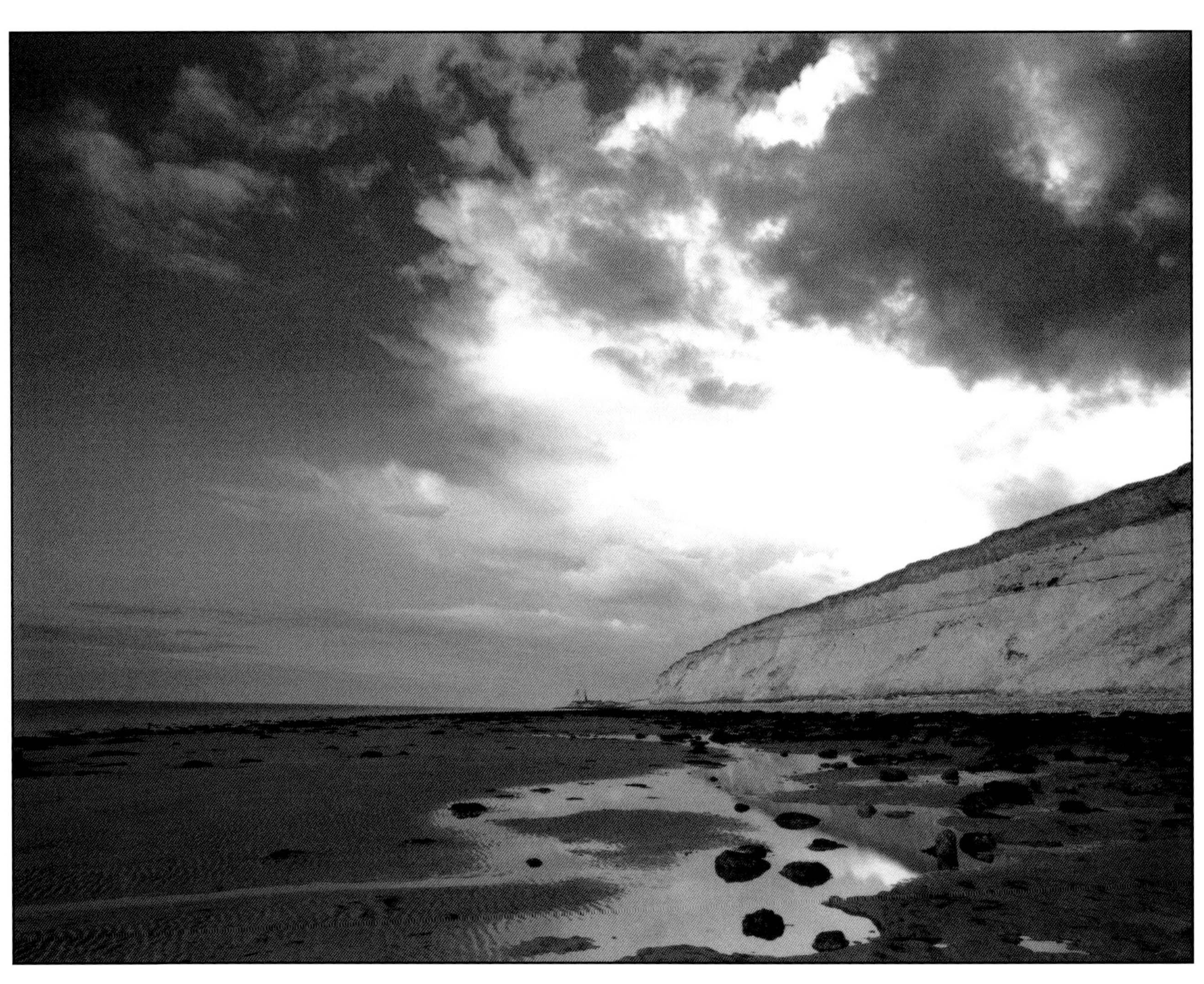

40
Reculver from Beltinge
1993

41
Twilight
Herne Common, 1995

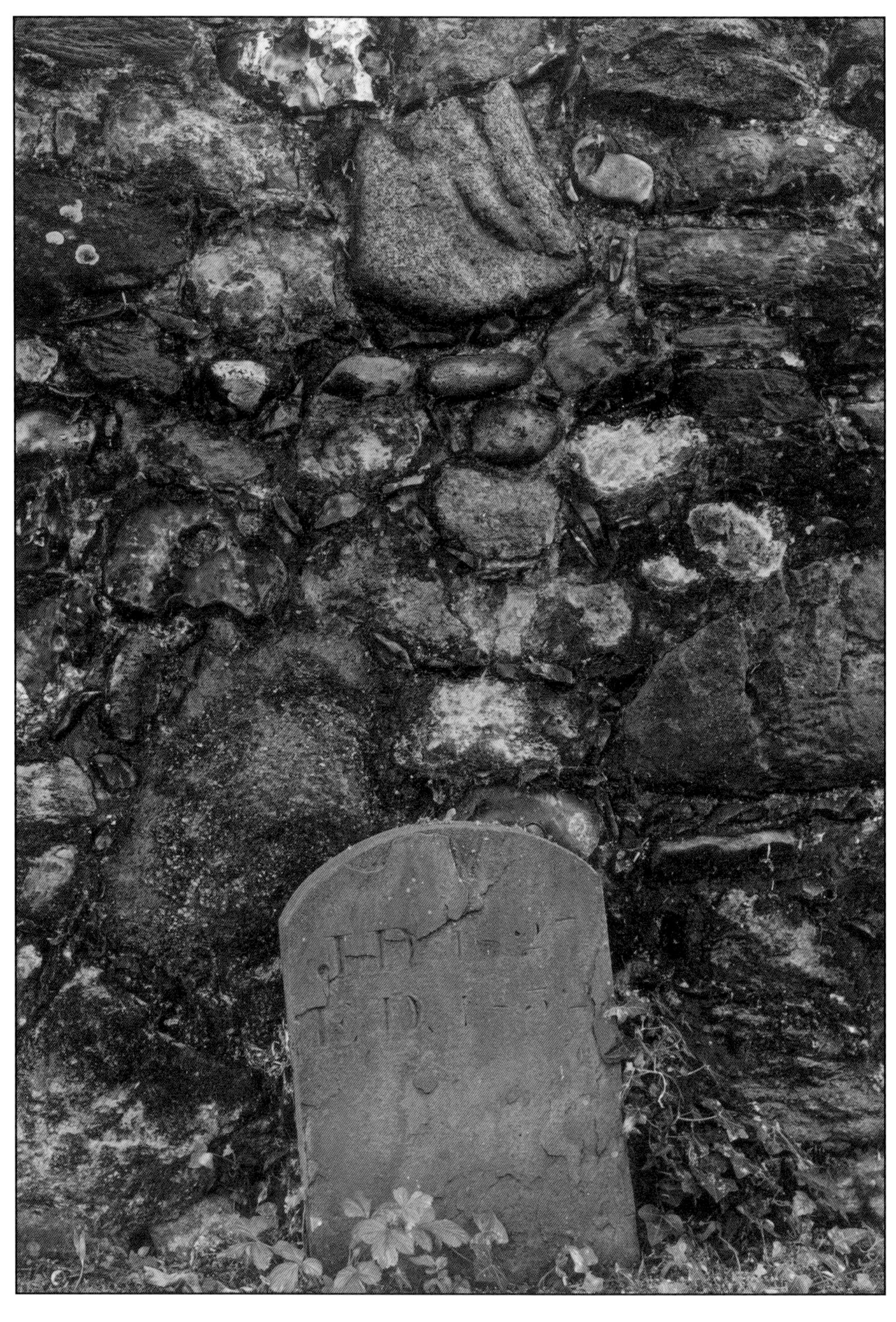

42

Headstone and flint wall

St Mary's Church, Sandwich, 1995

TECHNICAL DATA

Cameras

For the images in this portfolio, Trevor used the Konica T3 for 35mm, a Pentax 6x7 medium format slr, a Photox 6x9 field camera and more recently a Horseman 6x9 field camera. All light readings were made using a Pentax Spotmeter 5 fitted with a zone scale.

Lenses

Hexar and Hexanon lenses are used for the Konica system, and Rodenstock, Schneider and Nikon lenses are used for the field cameras.

Films

The film used for each exposure is shown in the table below, the key for which is as follows:

TMX	Kodak T-Max 100 rated at ISO 50
Delta100	Ilford Delta 100 rated at ISO 50
Delta400	Ilford Delta 400 rated at ISO 200
Kodak IR	Kodak infrared film (different ISOs depending on conditions)
Konica IR	Konica infrared film (different ISOs depending on conditions)

Development

Trevor uses various film/developer combinations and developer dilutions. The main developers used are Ilford Perceptol (1+3); Kodak HC110 (1+31); Paterson FX39 (1+9 or 1+14); Ilford LC29 (1+29 to 1+59).

Depending on the subject and lighting conditions, Trevor varies development to modify contrast. This is shown in the table below as:

N	normal contrast
N-	compacted contrast (soft)
N+	expanded contrast (hard)

Plate	*Format*	*Lens*	*Filter**	*Shutter†*	*Aperture*	*Film*	*Dev*	*Comments*
1	6x9	150	Y	1 sec	f/45	TMX	N	rising front
2	6x9	47	O	1/2	f/16	TMX	N-	rising front
3	6x9	100	Y	1/8	f/16	TMX	N-	front fall
4	6x9	75	O	2x1/2	f/32	Delta100	N-	rising front
5	6x9	47	O	1 sec	f/16	TMX	N-	rising front
6	6x9	150	Y	1/4	f/22	TMX	N-	rising front
7	6x9	100	UV	2x1/4	f/16	TMX	N-	rising front
8	6x7	35	R	1/2	f/16	TMX	N	–
9	6x9	100	O	1/8	f/16	TMX	N	rising front
10	6x7	135	UV	1 sec	f/16	TMX	N+	–
11	6x7	90	UV	1 sec	f/22	TMX	N-	–
12	6x7	90	UV	1/2	f/16	TMX	N-	–

Plate	*Format*	*Lens*	*Filter**	*Shutter†*	*Aperture*	*Film*	*Dev*	*Comments*
13	6x7	90	Y	1/2	f/22	TMX	N-	–
14	6x9	150	Y	1/4	f/16	TMX	N-	lens tilt
15	6x7	135	O	1/2	f/22	TMX	N	–
16	6x9	100	ND64	6 min	f/45	TMX	N-	–
17	6x7	100	Y	1/2	f/22	TMX	N	–
18	6x9	100	Y	1/2	f/22	TMX	N-	–
19	6x9	75	Y	1/2	f/22	Delta100	N-	–
20	6x9	100	O	5 sec	f/16	TMX	N-	–
21	6x9	100	O	2 sec	f/32	TMX	N-	–
22	6x9	75	Y	1 sec	f/22	Delta100	N+	rising front
23	6x7	90	UV	1/2	f/16	TMX	N+	–
24	6x9	100	UV	1 min	f/32	TMX	N+	–
25	6x9	100	UV	2 min	f/45	TMX	N+	front fall
26	35mm	28	R	1/125	f/8	Kodak IR	N	–
27	6x9	65	R	1/2	f/32	Konica IR	N+	rising front
28	6x9	100	UV	4 sec	f/45	Delta400	N	lens tilt
29	6x9	100	UV	1 sec	f/22	TMX	N-	–
30	6x9	100	UV	1 sec	f/22	TMX	N-	drop bed, lens tilt
31	6x9	75	UV	1 sec	f/22	Delta100	N-	back swung right
32	6x7	135	O	1/2	f/32	TMX	N	–
33	6x7	135	O	1/2	f/22	TMX	N+	–
34	6x7	135	O	1/2	f/22	TMX	N+	–
35	6x7	135	O	1/2	f/22	TMX	N+	–
36	6x9	150	Y	1/15	f/16	TMX	N	lens tilt
37	6x7	135	O	1/2	f/22	TMX	N+	–
38	6x9	150	Y	1/15	f/22	TMX	N-	rising front
39	6x9	47	UV	1/8	f/22	TMX	N	–
40	6x7	45	O	1/2	f/22	TMX	N	–
41	6x9	150	Y	1 sec	f/5.6	TMX	N	–
42	6x9	100	O	3 sec	f/16	TMX	N+	drop bed

* *key for filters: ND64 = 64x neutral density (B+W 1.8); O = orange; R = red; UV = ultra violet; Y = yellow.*
† *shutter speeds are shown as a fraction of a second except where otherwise stated.*
Plates 4 and 7 are double exposures in the camera.

For details of other titles in the Contemporary Portfolio series and a free catalogue of Creative Monochrome publications, please write to:
Creative Monochrome Ltd, 20 St Peters Road, Croydon, Surrey, CR0 1HD, England
(Tel: 0181-686 3282; Fax: 0181-681 0662; e-mail: roger@cremono.demon.co.uk)